W9-BAO-871

What They Are Saying About
The Joy Of Not Working

☆ "Ernie Zelinski helps others find time to live. *The Joy Of Not Working* is a light, folksy compendium of quips, tips, and cartoons, all focused on how to find meaning outside the office."

   - Fawn Fitter, Career Writer, Boston Herald

☆ "The book should be "must" reading for every pre-retiree who dreads the thought of boredom and inactivity in retirement."

   - Retirement Planning Journal, (Published By International Society of Retirement Planners, Rockville, Maryland)

☆ "In *The Joy Of Not Working*, Zelinski explains how to combat boredom, develop motivation, live for today, rethink the terms of financial independence, and redefine the meaning of fulfillment."

   - Don Oldenburg, Career Writer, Washington Post

☆ " *The Joy Of Not Working* is finding a niche next to *"What Color Is Your Parachute?"* - in other words, it is becoming a sort of career guide for the involuntarily downsized."

   - Quill & Quire Magazine

☆ "For all the time we spend craving leisure time, discussing it, dreaming about it and planning for it, few among us use it well .....This is where Ernie J. Zelinski comes in .... Zelinski has made leisure his life's work .... Indeed, he wrote the book on it."

   - Carol Smith, Columnist, Seattle Post-Intelligencer

☆ "The message is that leisure, not work, is critical to happiness, that life is fleeting, that the employment ruts we dig for ourselves blind us to life's pleasures. Zelinski points out that no one's dying words have ever included, " I wish I had worked more.""

   - Katherine Gay, Careers Section, Financial Post

☆ "Give this book to someone who has just retired or been laid off."

   - Ellen Roseman, Business Editor, Globe & Mail

☆ " *The Joy Of Not Working* provides an easy-to-read set of principles for aspects of work, leisure, and their intersections with personal values and happiness."

   - Contemporary Psychology - A Journal Of Reviews (Published by The American Psychological Association)

What They Are Saying About
The Joy Of Not Working

☆ "Long a curiosity to his more tradition-bound acquaintances, Zelinski decided six years ago that he ought to write about his lifestyle and philosophy of leisure. The resulting tome has become an underground sensation."

> *- Kenneth Kidd, Report On Business Magazine*

☆ "Thank you for writing such a neat book."

> *- Dr. Norm Nichol, Psychologist, Mesa, Arizona*

☆ "First, *The Joy Of Cooking.* Next, *The Joy Of Sex.* And now: *The Joy Of Not Working.* .... it forces one to re-evaluate priorities and strive for balance."

> *- Debra Cummings, Lifestyle Editor, Calgary Sun*

☆ "Your book has destroyed my joy of <u>NOT</u> reading. It is hard to put down and difficult not to smile or laugh."

> *- Yar Kunycia, Architect, New York*

☆ "Zelinski's book will appeal to readers wanting to make a change in their lives ..... My sister-in-law, recently retired from some 30 years as a teacher, couldn't put the book down."

> *- Paul Bennett, Book Editor, Victoria Times Colonist*

☆ "Focusing on how to make life richer in spirit, Zelinski notes that people who do what they like doing generally end up happier than those whose goals are purely financial."

> *- Jeff Rowe, The Orange County Register, California*

☆ "Being a retired teacher of 41 years, I'd like to tell you this book *"The Joy Of Not Working"* is one of the best in content and presentation that I have read."

> *- Lois Auger, Park Falls, Wisconsin*

☆ "I urge you to check your local library or bookstore for a copy of this highly entertaining and thought-provoking book .... *The Joy Of Not Working* is one of the best how-to books I have found."

> *- Don McClenahan, Alumni Newsletter Editor for WMI Inc., Oak Brook, Illinois*

☆ "You think your job is tough - try trading with Ernie Zelinski. His job is not working, and he's been doing it successfully for the last 14 years."

> *- Keiko Ohnuma, Business Writer, Oakland Tribune*

The

Joy

Of

Not Working

How To Enjoy Your Leisure Time Like Never Before

Ernie J. Zelinski

VIP BOOKS

Visions International Publishing

Edmonton, Alberta, Canada

VIP BOOKS Edition

Published by Visions International Publishing
Edmonton, Alberta, Canada

Seventh printing, May, 1994 by:

Art Design Printing Inc., Edmonton, Alberta, Canada

Cover design and illustration by Vern Busby

COPYRIGHT © 1991, 1993 by Ernie J. Zelinski
ALL RIGHTS RESERVED.

Reproduction in whole or in part, by any means, is not
allowed without written permission from the copyright
holder.

Direct any inquiries to:

Ernie J. Zelinski   Telephone (403) 436-1798
P.O Box 4072, Edmonton, Alberta, Canada, T6E 4S8

Canadian Cataloguing in Publication Data

Zelinski, Ernie J. (Ernie John), 1949-
   The joy of not working

   ISBN 0-9694194-1-4

   1. Leisure. 2. Work ethic. 3. Self-actualization
(Psychology). I. Title.

   GV174.Z44 1991   790'.01'35   C91-091350-1

This book is dedicated to you, the reader. I hope you will use the principles from *The Joy Of Not Working* to enhance your life as well as contribute to a better world in which we live.

Table Of Contents

Important - Disclaimer

The purpose of this book is to inform, educate, challenge, and entertain the reader. The book's content is not meant to be a substitute for any professional services.

This book is sold with the understanding that neither the author nor the publisher is engaged in rendering legal, psychological, medical, or any other professional advice. If such advice or other assistance is required, the personal services of competent professionals should be found.

Any decisions made by the reader as a result of reading this book are made at the sole responsibility of the reader. The author and publisher assume no liability for any such decisions.

Preface

This book is designed to make you a winner.

Unlike most how-to books on winning, this book is not a book about winning at a job or making money. Neither is it a book about winning at competitive games. This book is about winning when you are not working, in a way that is not competitive, but is still very rewarding.

You're a winner when you have a zest for life. You're a winner when you wake up every morning excited about the day. You're a winner when you enjoy doing what you're doing. And you're a winner when you pretty well know what you want to do with your life.

> "Everything has been figured out except how to live."
>
> - Jean-Paul Sartre

Whether you are retired, unemployed, or working, you can use *The Joy Of Not Working* as the practical and reliable guide to creating a paradise away from the workplace. Because all of us from time to time need reminders about the obvious and not-so obvious, we can use a handy guide for enhancing our leisure time.

This book is the result of my education, an education which has nothing to do with the curricula in place at schools and universities. It is an education I acquired through my personal experiences, far removed from my formal education.

> "Education is very admirable but let us not forget that anything worth knowing cannot be taught."
>
> - Oscar Wilde

Over ten years ago, at the age of 29, I embarked on a new career. Having lost my job, I decided I would be a creative loafer for a year or so. Although my being without a regular job was supposed to be temporary, I have yet to return to a regular job.

1

In my last regular job I allowed myself to be imprisoned by a system which is not designed for free spirits. For almost six years I worked for a government-owned utility, where I was supposed to work from nine to five. The nine-to-five job was more often an eight-to-six job with weekend work. Most of this extra time at work was without extra compensation.

Not having taken a vacation for over three years, I decided to take ten weeks of vacation one summer. Aside from the fact I did not have approval from my superiors, this was a great idea. I really enjoyed those ten weeks. The idea was so brilliant that I ended up fired from my job as a professional engineer. The verdict was I had violated company policy by taking the extended vacation.

Obviously my superiors did not like what I had done. Despite my high performance evalutions and my not having taken a vacation for some time, the company terminated my employment when I returned to work. I am not sure if my termination was solely because of my violating company policy. Perhaps my superiors were envious of how much I enjoyed myself during my extended vacation. Many supervisors, especially those in government, don't like having to deal with subordinates who are enjoying themselves.

> *"What's the use of being a genius if you can't use it as an excuse for being unemployed."*
>
> *- Gerald Barzan*

For the first few weeks I was bitter about being fired. Having been a dedicated and productive worker, I knew I had made many important contributions to this company. There was obviously a great injustice done because they fired an indispensible employee.

A big turning point for me was the day when I realized my firing was a blessing in disguise. Along with reluctantly admitting I was not indispensible, I lost interest in a regular nine-to-five job. I wanted to make sure that I took as much time off as I could from then on, especially in summers. A normal job was out of the question.

My career as a professional engineer was over. For the next two years I didn't work at all, nor did I attend any educational institution. My purpose in life was to be happy without a job.

What did I do during this time? Although at times I had very little money, I lived what I consider to be a very prosperous life. I engaged in many constructive and satisfying activities too numerous to mention. The main point is I celebrated life. I grew as a person and went through a transformation in my values. It was during these two years that I truly earned my Doctorate in Leisure (which no university has as yet granted me).

Mr. Zelinski, Harvard University, always thankful for all major contributions to society, today would like to grant you an honorary degree of Doctor in Leisure.

After those two years of total leisure, I decided I wouldn't work in any month that doesn't have an "r" in it. To me, May, June, July, and August are too suited for leisure activities. In fact, because I enjoy my free time so much, I have successfully avoided a regular nine-to-five job for the last twelve years. For all intents and purposes, I have been in temporary retirement or semi-retirement since I was 29 years old.

Over the years many people have asked me how I am able to utilize so much leisure time without getting bored. From talking to these people, I realized many individuals have problems with how they can get satisfaction in their spare time. One day it also occurred to me that there has been very little written on how to manage leisure time.

That is when the idea for this book was conceived. Since I believe anyone can take responsibility, and fill their spare time with constructive and exciting activities, I decided a book could help many people.

In the following chapters I will share my thoughts about leisure, along with a number of my experiences. To give a much broader perspective to leisure, I am not drawing only on my own experiences. A greater part of this book is the result of studying and listening to the stories, experiences, and aspirations of other people.

This book is not a highly academic one. I have tried to avoid great detail and academic jargon which most readers wouldn't enjoy. Instead, I have tried to make the book as short as possible, so that the message is presented with the fewest possible words. The book's format encompasses text, exercises, cartoons, diagrams, and quotations to appeal to the many learning styles that individuals have. This format was used in my first book. The many positive comments I received from people who read *The Art Of Seeing Double Or Better In Business* convinced me this format works best in getting the message across in an interesting and entertaining way.

"The life of Riley" has been a popular expression for decades. A person living the life of Riley is one able to live comfortably without working. This book is about how you can live the life of Riley; what it takes to live the life of Riley may surprise you.

> *"Success is a matter of luck, just ask any failure."*
>
> *- Anon*

Success at leisure is not based on being lucky in life. It takes effort in following and applying certain relevant principles; these principles are the basis for this book. By following these principles, you will be able to discover and choose some new directions in your life. With these new directions, you will be on the road to many wonderful and fulfilling experiences, which you could never experience at any job. You will be able to claim, as I am able, that you can be much happier away from the workplace than at the workplace.

If you want to add to the tone, quality, and experience in your life, this book should be a valuable asset. I trust the *The Joy Of Not Working* will entertain, challenge, influence, and motivate you to attain an exciting and rewarding life of leisure.

Ernie J. Zelinski

1. You Too Can Live The Life Of Riley

A Grand Time To Loaf

On the second day he was visiting a large city, a wealthy and somewhat eccentric traveler encountered six panhandlers, who all had been soliciting money the day before. The panhandlers now were all lying in the sun. Obviously taking a break from the duties related to their chosen profession, the panhandlers all looked up as the traveler approached.

The traveler decided to have some fun. He offered a $1000 bill to the one who could prove that he was the laziest panhandler. Five panhandlers jumped up to take part in the contest, all hoping to claim the prize. Each one proceeded to demonstrate in varying ways, such as by sitting down while soliciting money from other tourists, how much lazier he could be at his panhandling than his colleagues.

> *"I am a friend of the workingman, and I would rather be his friend, than be one."*
>
> *- Clarence Darrow*

After an hour, having watched the five competitive ones with amusement, the traveler made his decision and awarded the $1000 bill. He concluded that the sixth panhandler, who had refrained from the competition, was definitely the laziest. The sixth panhandler had remained lying on the grass, reading a paper and enjoying the sun.

There is a moral to this story: Not working, when it is more appropriate to enjoy yourself loafing, can have its benefits.

This book is about the benefits to be enjoyed while away from the workplace. It is about how you, if retired, can manage and enhance your large amount of spare time. It is about how you, if presently

5

unemployed, can enjoy your extra spare time while in between jobs. It is about how you, if employed, can better enjoy your limited spare time.

In other words, no matter what your situation, this book is about how you can get more satisfaction and pleasure from your leisure. Welcome to "the joy of not working."

Leisure: The Opposite Of Work But Not Quite

"How do you define leisure?" This is an interesting, but difficult question. The question was posed to me by a participant in a leisure-planning seminar which I presented at the Canadian Association of Pre-retirement Planners' 1990 Conference.

Not having a definite answer, I decided to follow one of my many principles of creativity: give the problem away. I delegated by asking the other seminar participants to define leisure.

After much discussion we arrived at what appeared to be a consensus. We ended up defining leisure as "spare time over and above the time required to perform the necessities in life." This was good enough so we could continue.

Of course, this definition can in itself lead to another good question: "What do you define as necessities in life?" Eating may be a necessity, but casual dining for an hour or two at a bistro is not a necessity. This is a pleasure in life. Casual dining is one of my favorite leisure activities. To others, eating is a necessity, and a bothersome activity.

Later I looked up the definition of leisure in several dictionaries. Dictionaries commonly define leisure as "time free from required work in which a person may rest, amuse oneself, and do the things one likes to do."

So where does eating fit into the dictionaries'

Dictionary

lei-sure *(le'zher or lezh'er),* n. 1. the opposite of work but not quite. 2. Somewhat of a paradox. 3. What a person does living the life of Riley. - adj. and adv. **lei'sure-ly.**

lem-on *(lem/un)* n. 1. a small tropical fruit with pale-yellow skin and very acid juice; 2. the tree, related to the orange, which bears this fruit; 3. a pale yellow colour: - Adj

lem-on-ade *(lem'un-ad)* n. a drink of sweetened water flavoured with lemon juice.

definition? Is eating work? Is eating leisure? Or is eating something altogether different? I wasn't about to take the time to locate the people responsible for the dictionaries' definition to see if they could clarify this confusion. I suspect they would have great difficulty in doing this for me.

> *"I hate definitions."*
> *- Benjamin Disraeli*

After much thought, I was still a little puzzled. How can I define leisure to prevent the potential for endless questioning at my seminars? I just want to present my ideas on how to enjoy leisure. I don't want to be a philosopher to determine whether eating is leisure, or leisure is eating.

Then I concluded the purpose for my seminars (and this book) is not to establish a universal and perfect definition for leisure. Leisure will always mean different things to different people. However, leisure, loosely defined, is the time an individual spends away from work to do the things he or she wants to do. It is up to you and me to define what is work and what is leisure for our own personal needs. After that, it is up to you and me to do whatever is necessary to find out what we as individuals like to do. Then we have to do it.

Is this leisure or is it work?

Doing it is easier said than done. There is an interesting paradox here: The paradox is that leisure is about not working; however, to attain satisfaction at our leisure we will have to "work" at it. As odd as it may seem, leisure is the opposite of work, but something that may require a great deal of it.

The Illusions Of Leisure, Retirement, And Lotteries

By choice or by chance, all of us sooner or later have to deal with how to use and enjoy leisure time. There is no doubt that what we do with our spare time will determine the quality of our lives.

"It is paradoxical but nonetheless true that the nearer man comes to his goal to make his life easy and abundant, the more he undermines the foundations of a meaningful existence."

- Franz Alexander

Because it was once a rather rare commodity, leisure was considered a luxury for many centuries. Only recently has leisure become abundant enough to a point where some people now expect to experience decades of it through lengthy retirement.

Leisure time in great measure is the ultimate goal of many North Americans. Everyone desires at least a certain amount. Some claim their goal is to have nothing but leisure on their hands, so they can live the life of Riley. Yet many people are not prepared for handling substantial leisure time. Sustained leisure has become a burden to many, even though they are in a financial position to choose and healthy enough to enjoy it.

Most of us reserve the enjoyment of leisure for the future; often the future arrives too soon. We end up with much more spare time due to retirement or job layoffs. The reality then is we have time in large amounts to spend on leisure activities. Reality is often quite sobering. Whether we have found our jobs exciting and stimulating, or boring and depressing, many of us are in for a big surprise.

Faculty Of Leisure Studies

Leisure without problems is one of life's illusions. Once we have an increase in our leisure time, many of us are faced with new problems to replace the old. Various studies confirm that many people have difficulty in handling spare time.

One study by the Department of Commerce in the United States reported that only 58 percent of people were getting "a great deal" of satisfaction from how they spend their leisure time. This means that 42 percent of individuals could use substantial help in enhancing the quality in their leisure. Even some of the people getting a great deal of satisfaction may not be getting as much satisfaction as they would like. Many of these people probably could use some help as well.

The majority of us will spend the greater part of our adult lives working. Taking into account getting ready for work, commuting to work, talking about our jobs, and worrying about getting laid off, we will have spent more time during our working lives thinking about work, than thinking about all our other concerns in life.

Associated with thinking about work is thinking about how great it will be when we don't have to work anymore. Many of us dream about how much better things will be when we have much more leisure time. When I worked as an engineer, I was amazed (and dejected) to hear young engineers and technicians in their 20's spend a lot of time talking about pensions and retirement. Quite frankly, in my 20's I had many more interesting things to talk about. (If you are interested in what they were, buy me dinner and we'll have a most interesting conversation.)

> *"Oh to reach the point of death and realize one has not lived at all."*
>
> - Thoreau

Society influences us to believe that retirement and happiness are one and the same. Retirement is supposed to mean a life with fulfillment through enjoyable and rewarding activities. It is supposed to be the great escape from the stresses inherent in most jobs.

Up until a few years ago I, like most people in my generation, allowed myself to be influenced by the general thinking prevalent in society. I believed that retirement and increased leisure were something everyone would look forward to, and enjoy once they attained it.

Since then I have learned it is dangerous, more often than not, to accept the teachings and thinking most people in society adopt. The masses are frequently wrong. Certain factions in society regularly sell us a false bill of goods. We are not given the complete picture; the finer things in life often turn out differently from what society has led us to believe.

> *"There are two tragedies in life; not getting what you want and getting it."*
>
> - Oscar Wilde

Being unable to retire can be a tragedy. So can attaining retirement. People nearing retirement have fears about imminent diminished purpose and activity. Once retirement is taken, the results can be negative to the point of being tragic. It isn't uncommon for death or senility to occur within two years; even suicide is possible. In fact, the suicide rate for American men is four times higher in retirement than in any stage in life.

Winning a major lottery in North America is supposed to be an event which enhances our lifes to immeasurable levels. Becoming a millionaire should give us the life about which we have always dreamed. Not all evidence supports these notions.

A major lottery winner in New York expressed regret after having quit his job. "I really miss that truck driving. The biggest loss of my life is not having someone to tell me what to do." These were the words echoed by a millionaire ex-trucker as reported in the book, *Suddenly Rich.* The book's authors, Jerry LeBlanc and Rena Dictor LeBlanc, studied wealthy people who had acquired sudden fortunes.

Guess I'll apply for work again. After having been retired for six months, I am really looking forward to returning to the misery of a job.

The LeBlancs found certain people with sustained leisure were not very happy. After having been given a mandatory routine by employers for so long, they had trouble dealing with days totally lacking in structure and purpose. Many other lottery winners continued to work, despite harassment from co-workers and friends, about keeping a job which they didn't need for financial purposes.

A study by Challenger, Gray & Christmas Inc. found that over 50 percent of people accepting early retirement packages were more than happy to return to work after they had spent more than three months in retirement. Retirement was not what many people thought it would be. A life comprising total leisure wasn't all that enjoyable. With all its negatives, work wasn't so bad after all.

Two Sides To Taking It Easy

For many people the life associated with taking it easy is difficult to handle. Living the life of Riley may not have been easy even for Riley. To the unprepared, having spare time in great amounts can bring on many anxieties.

"If a man could have just half of his wishes, he would double his troubles."

- Benjamin Franklin

You may have the same difficulties if you don't put in the effort to develop your ability to enjoy leisure activities. If you haven't developed a love for leisure by the time you retire, you may feel the life of Riley is the biggest ripoff since the last time you bought the Brooklyn Bridge.

Here are some common problems that people have with their leisure time:

- ⇨ Boredom with oneself and others
- ⇨ No real satisfaction from leisure activities
- ⇨ All dressed up and nowhere to go
- ⇨ All dressed up, somewhere to go, but no one with whom to go
- ⇨ Friction with spouse when time together increases
- ⇨ Not enough things to do
- ⇨ So much to do and no time to do it
- ⇨ Hard time deciding what to do
- ⇨ Bankroll of a peasant but tastes of a millionaire
- ⇨ Bankroll of a millionaire but poverty consciousness of a peasant
- ⇨ Feeling guilty about having fun and enjoying oneself
- ⇨ Enjoyment from only those things illegal, immoral, or unhealthy

The other side to leisure is much more positive. Unlimited leisure time can be a great reward in life. Many people are able to adjust to a life of total leisure, without missing a stride. To some, the leisurely life is even more than they expected. They have become more active than ever before. Each day is a new adventure. These people will tell you nothing can be as enjoyable as a leisurely lifestyle.

When you get to enjoy leisure time to the fullest, your life will be enhanced to immeasurable levels. Success at handling leisure will contribute to a life about which many on this earth can only dream. Some benefits available to you from an increase in your leisure are:

☆ A higher quality of life
☆ Personal growth
☆ Improved health
☆ Higher self-esteem
☆ Less stress and a more relaxed lifestyle
☆ Satisfaction from challenging activities
☆ Excitement and adventure
☆ A more balanced lifestyle if employed
☆ A sense of self-worth even if unemployed
☆ Quality of family life increases

The difference between success and failure at anything is often slim.

The difference between success and failure at anything is often slim. Having covered the problems and benefits of leisure, let's look at what is essential for our receiving as many benefits as possible from our leisure time.

The following exercise is just one of several you will encounter in the book. You will get a lot more from this book if you take the time to attempt all the exercises. You can add to the answers, where a choice of answers is given, and none is suitable to you.

Exercise #1-1 - The Essentials

Which of the factors below are essential for attaining success at managing and enjoying leisure time?

- Excellent health
- Living in an exciting city
- Having many friends from different walks of life
- A charming personality
- Owning a motorhome
- A love for travel
- Athletic ability
- Good looks
- Excellent physical condition
- Financial independence
- A beach cabin
- Living in a warm climate
- Having had good parents
- A great marriage or relationship
- Having many hobbies

Before we discuss what is essential, let's look at two individuals who are having trouble with leisure, and one who isn't. This gives us a better indication of what is essential for attaining satisfaction in leisure.

The Life Of Riley Can Be Elusive

Recently I talked to Delton, who is 67 years old, financially secure, and plays tennis (sometimes better than I do) at the club where I play. Although Delton liked the company he worked with for many years, he did not like its policy on mandatory retirement at 65.

When he first retired, he had no idea about what he should do with his time. He was lost. Delton, two years into retirement, is now happy his

> *"People waste more time waiting for someone to take charge of their lives than they do in any other pursuit."*
>
> *- Gloria Steinem*

company allows him to work part time. His time away from the job is not well spent (except when he whips me in a game of tennis). Delton even confided with me that he hasn't liked weekends for a long time. He has always had a hard time deciding what to do on his days off.

> *"The only thing some people do is grow older."*
>
> *- Ed Howe*

Rich, whom I also met at the same tennis club, is another example of someone who had problems with his spare time. The difference between Delton and Rich is that Rich yearned to retire early. Like many people in the city in which I live, Rich fantasized about moving to the west coast to live the life of Riley. Rich got his wish when he was only 44. Having worked with a police force since he was 19, Rich was able to retire with a decent pension after working only 25 years.

After Rich moved away to the west coast to enjoy the life of Riley, he realized that he must not have too much in common with Riley. Rich found handling unlimited spare time extremely difficult. He responded by opening a business. When he lost his shirt on that venture (not serious - you don't need a shirt in west coast weather), he tried several other things, including going back to work for a short time. Rich is still undecided on how he can best deal with retirement. This is somewhat unfortunate, considering Rich is in an enviable position to which many people aspire.

Unemployed Stockbroker Lives Life Of Riley

In 1987 North American newspapers reported on the plight of stockbrokers, who were having it tough after the October 19, 1987 market crash. Young executives, who had known a bull market and the expensive lifestyles it brought, were bewildered and astounded. Many, who were about to lose their jobs paying them $200,000 to $500,000 a year, were saying they couldn't take other jobs at $100,000 a year, because their expenses were too high. (I'm sure these stories brought tears to many readers' eyes as they did to mine.)

> *"With an evening coat and a white tie, anybody, even a stockbroker, can gain a reputation for being civilized."*
>
> *- Oscar Wilde*

Of course, it would have been unthinkable for these stockbrokers to consider unemployment for a few months or a year. Due to their expensive lifestyles, the alternative of temporarily being without a job and income didn't enter their minds.

My friend Denny was a stockbroker during the period before the crash. He hadn't been a top producer and had saved very little money. After the crash, Denny left the business altogether. He didn't immediately go looking for another job (not even a low paying one at $100,000 a year). Although Denny had very little money to live the life of Riley, he decided to take it easy for at least a year so he could enjoy a different lifestyle.

During the time Denny was unemployed, I saw a person who was as content as anyone could be in this world. He was relaxed, he had a smile he couldn't lose, and he was a treat to be around because of his positive nature. I knew many working people who were making good money at their high status jobs, but I didn't know one working person who was as happy as Denny. He took the better part of a year to live the life of Riley.

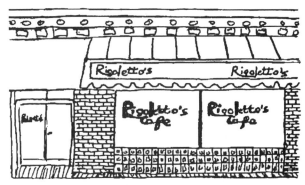

If you can't enjoy the great restaurants of the world, you will have a hard time living the life of Riley.

Denny has since returned to the workforce in another city. On a visit back to my home city, Denny mentioned that although he was enjoying his new career, he was yearning for the time when he again could take a year or two off just to enjoy life. There is no doubt in my mind that Denny, unlike Rich and Delton, will enjoy the life of Riley when he permanently retires.

Riley's Secret

No matter who you are, you can experience the many joys of not working. I can say this simply because I personally have been able to be as happy, if not happier, not working as working. If I can do it, so can you. My firsthand experience at spending over half of my adult years without a job has given me an insight as to what it takes to be a success away from the job. My success has been the result of my paying attention to what I must do to be happy at leisure, and then being creative in doing it.

> *"Do what you can, with what you have, where you are."*
>
> *- Theodore Roosevelt*

The point is that I haven't been blessed with any special talents and abilities which you don't have. Other people like Denny, who experience great enjoyment in their spare time, also don't have any special talents or abilities with which they were born. Success in life's adventures doesn't come from having some huge advantage over others. We all have the ability required to make life a success; the key is to acknowledge our own talents, and to use them.

So then, what are the differences between people who are able to live the life of Riley, and those who can't? Why is my friend Denny so content with having nothing but free time on his hands, while my two acquaintances, Delton and Rich, find unlimited free time a burden?

Let's return to Exercise #1-1 on page 13. If you chose any item which was on the list, you are a victim of your own incorrect thinking about what it takes to master leisure. Not one item which I listed is essential for successfully living the life of Riley. Every item on the list may be an asset, but none is essential.

> *"They are able because they think they are able."*
>
> *-Virgil*

I want to stress that we can discount financial independence as an essential item. Delton and Rich are much better off financially than Denny was. If financial independence is essential, we should have Delton and Rich happy in their leisure, and Denny unhappy in his, rather than the other way around. In Chapter 11 we will look at what role money plays in the enjoyment of leisure time.

Then what is essential? The life of Riley is nothing more than a state of mind. Denny has the one essential ingredient - a healthy attitude. Riley himself had to have a healthy attitude to live the good life about which people talked. Nothing can replace a good attitude for success in life. If you don't have a healthy attitude, then you must put in the effort to develop one. This book is mainly about developing and maintaining such an attitude.

2. What You See Is What You Get

Thinking For A Change

We can change the quality of our lives by changing the context in which we view our circumstances. Two people can be faced with the same situation, such as being fired from a job. Yet one will view it as a blessing, and the other will view it as a curse. Changing the context of the situation depends on our ability to challenge and be flexible in our thinking.

Most of us do not take the time to reflect upon what we are thinking, and why. To produce change in our thinking, we must start thinking for a change.

By challenging our thinking, we set the stage for fresh perspectives and new values to replace outmoded beliefs. Challenging the way we think about work and its benefits helps us develop a healthy attitude about leisure. Never challenging the way we think has at least two inherent dangers:

> *"Most people think only once or twice a year. I have made myself an international reputation by thinking once or twice a week."*
>
> *- George Bernard Shaw*

⇨   The first danger is we may get locked into one way of thinking, without seeing other alternatives which may be more appropriate.

⇨   The second danger is we may adopt a set of values which at the time makes a lot of sense. Time will pass; with time, things will change. The original values will no longer be appropriate because of the changes, but we will still continue to function with the original, outmoded values.

●

Old Dogs Can Learn New Tricks

Draw a black dot like the one above on a whiteboard and ask a class of adult students what they see. Practically everyone will say they see a black dot, and only a black dot. Place a similar dot in front of a class of children in grade school, and the answers will excite you. You will hear interesting things like:

- darkness outside a round window
- a black bear rolled up in a ball
- a hubcap
- a horse's eye
- a black marble
- the inside of a pipe
- a chocolate cookie

> *"Grown-ups never understand anything by themselves, and it is tiresome for children to be always and forever explaining things to them."*
>
> *- From The Little Prince by Antoine de Saint Exupery*

We all come into this world blessed with great imaginations. As children, we all have the capacity and flexibility to see the world from many different points of view. Because we pay attention to practically everything around us, our ability to enjoy life is remarkable.

At some point in childhood, most of us start to lose these abilities. Society and our parents influence us by telling us what we should expect. We are conditioned to look for acceptance. To be accepted socially, we stop questioning. We lose our mental flexibility and we stop paying attention.

The result is our thinking becomes very structured. Structured beliefs and values lend themselves to erroneous, incomplete, or outdated perceptions. These distorted perceptions interfere with our creativity and enjoyment of life.

18

Being creative goes hand in hand with having a healthy attitude. In any field of endeavor, creative people are the ones who are most successful over the long term. They see opportunity, where others see insurmountable problems.

What's the matter Mitch? Did you lose all of your creativity when you turned 55? Use what I use to get out of these situations!

Researchers have found that the major difference between creative people and uncreative people is creative people simply think they are creative. The uncreative have become too structured and routinized in their thinking, and erroneously don't think of themselves as having what it takes to be creative.

Imperative to having a healthy attitude is realizing that we have to continually challenge our perceptions to avoid inhabiting the world of delusions. People who don't develop a habit of carefully examining their own premises and beliefs run the risk of seeing a world which has little relationship to reality. The results of this destructive practice can be serious, ranging from disappointments to depression to mental illness.

Some people are uncomfortable with the notion that their own attitudes and beliefs are all that stop them from achieving success. Most frightening to them is having to give up their excuses for not winning in the game of life. My observation is people, who most resist change, as well as resist accepting their perceptions may be wrong, are those who most need to change their perceptions to get their lives back on track to fulfillment.

> *"The dog too old to learn new tricks always has been."*
>
> *- Anon*

Old dogs can learn new tricks, if they want to learn them. The only thing that can stop any one of us from learning new behaviors is ourselves. Age is commonly used as an excuse. The age-old excuse of age has always been used by people who became structured in their thinking at an early age.

In other words, their attitude and resistance to change - not their chronological age - have interfered with their ability to change. People who maintain their flexibility in thinking in adulthood are not hindered by age when it comes to developing new values and behaviors.

In The Land Of The Blind One Eye Is King

Exercise #2-1 - The Three Secrets To Fulfillment

You're telling me, "Life is a joke!" Is that all there is to enlightenment?

A successful, but unhappy American entrepreneur had acquired a lot of wealth. He decided to retire and take it easy; however, he soon realized he was still not very happy.

Because his life was so empty, the entrepreneur decided to go in search of a Zen master who knew three important secrets about how to live life to the fullest. After twenty months of searching, the entrepreneur finally found this Zen master high on top of an obscure mountain.

The Zen master was happy to reveal the three secrets to having a happy and satisfying life. The entrepreneur was surprised at what he was told.

What were the three secrets?

⇨   1. _____

⇨   2. _____

⇨   3. _____

One of the keys to enjoying the world more is to practice the habit of flexibility. There is an old French proverb: "In the land of the blind, one eye is king." Being flexible will allow you to see things in this world which others don't see.

For the above exercise, were you able to come up with the three secrets to fulfillment in life? According to the Zen master they are: (1) pay attention, (2) pay attention, and (3) pay attention.

> *"Only the most foolish of mice would hide in a cat's ear. But only the wisest of cats would think to look there."*
>
> *- Scott Love*

One important thing creative people do is pay attention to the world around them. In general, creative people see a lot of opportunity in life. Uncreative people focus on the lack of opportunity, due to their inability to pay attention.

For a fulfilling life, learn to truly pay attention. The way to develop a healthy attitude is to develop your ability to focus your attention and consciousness on new things. You should also develop fresh ways of perceiving familiar things. If you are a rigid person, you will require effort, along with courage, to change your perceptions, so you can start experiencing life and leisure in new ways.

Without giving it much thought, some people will say that the management and enjoyment of leisure time is nothing more than common sense. I couldn't agree with this point of view more. Then why do I have to write a book based on a lot of common sense? The reason is many people will go through extremes to complicate their lives, when following the basics will do. In other words, common sense is not very common.

Are You Paying Attention?

> *"The obscure we see eventually. The completely obvious, it seems, takes longer."*
>
> *- Edward R. Murrow*

All of us, to some degree, are not paying attention. We allow our perceptions to be affected by our voices of judgment. The result is we don't see all there is to see.

Do the four exercises on the following two pages as a test of your perception and ability to pay attention. See if you have the presence of mind to see everything there is to see. Allow yourself a few minutes for doing all the exercises.

Exercise #2-2 - Looking At Perception

Look at the following two figures and then continue
on to the other exercises.

Figure #1

A bird in the the hand	is worth two in the ditch

Figure #2

Exercise #2-3 - Triangles Galore

The diagram on the right is a perspective builder. You simply have to count the number of triangles in the diagram.

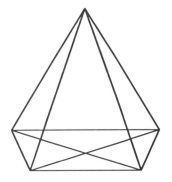

Exercise #2-4 - Playing With Matches

The equation on the right is made from matchsticks. Each line in the characters is one matchstick.

This equation is wrong. Move just one matchstick to make the equation correct.

Exercise #2-5 - Cycle Designed By A Psycho?

Although my undergraduate degree is in electrical engineering, a little while ago I decided to design something mechanical. This is a design for a new tandem bicycle that I created to help people enjoy leisure. (I know you are impressed.)

Analyze the merits of this design for a new bicycle.

A New Tandem Bicycle

Perception Is Everything

If you saw everything there was to see in Figure #1 of Exercise #2-2, you should have read the following in the two boxes.

A bird in **the the** hand is worth two in the ditch.

Not seeing the two "the's" shows you are not seeing all there is to see. You may be doing the same thing by overlooking all there is to see when solving your problems in life.

In Figure #2 you probably saw a triangle which is whiter than the rest of the page. First, note that there is no actual triangle drawn there. Your eyes just imagined one being there based on the other figures. In addition, the whiteness of this mirage triangle is no brighter than the rest of the page. Just as you saw a triangle and brightness that weren't in this figure, you may be seeing many things in life that aren't there. These can be imagined barriers to solving your problems.

In Exercise #2-3 most people see fewer than 25 triangles in the figure. Did you see all there was to see? There are 35 triangles. In doing Exercise #2-4, you should have generated a solution. If you did, that's great. However, if you stopped after only one solution, that's not so great. I have at least 12 solutions to this exercise (you can get these by attending my seminars). If you generate only one solution to your problems at work or play, you are missing out on the opportunity to generate more exciting and effective solutions.

> *Some men see things as they are and ask, "Why?" I see them as they have never been and ask, "Why not?"*
>
> *- George Bernard Shaw*

What did you think about my bicycle in Exercise #2-5? If your points were all negative, you have not explored my design fully. Unless you put down some positive points and some negative points, you have jumped to conclusions without due consideration to my "wonderful" design. Your voice of judgment has stepped in too soon. You should have considered positive points such as the rear wheel can be used as a spare in case the front tire goes flat. How about a more comfortable ride due to two back wheels? This bicycle could also have an advantage over conventional ones for carrying heavy loads; it will be great for overweight people. People may want to buy it as a status symbol because it is a new and different design. There are many positive and negative points to be

24

made for this design. To fully explore the merits of this design, you should consider all these points. Similarly, in evaluating your ideas or someone's suggestions, you should look at all positive and negative points, before making a decision.

In life, perception is everything; what you see is what you get. You can be the judge of how well you paid attention on the previous exercises. If you didn't see all there was to see, you may want to start paying more attention to the world around you.

Only The Foolish And Dead Don't Change

Today's world is changing at an unprecedented pace. To deal effectively with this change, your opinions, beliefs, and values shouldn't be carved in stone. Avoid being a rigid person and your life will be a lot easier in today's rapidly changing world.

Some people think changing values, beliefs, or opinions represents weakness. On the contrary, the ability to change represents strength by those willing to change and grow in life. There is much to be said for the saying that only the foolish and dead never change their beliefs and opinions. As I implied before, no matter who you are, you can change.

> *"Faced with having to change our views or prove that there is no need to do so, most of us immediately get busy on the proof."*
>
> *- John Kenneth Galbraith*

I want to stress that the more inflexible and less perceptual you are, the more problems you will have in living and adjusting to our rapidly changing world. My experience in teaching creativity seminars reveals that people who most need to change their thinking are most resistant to change. The opposite is true with highly adaptive and creative people. To them, change is exciting. They are always willing to challenge their points of view, and they are willing to change them when necessary.

Looking past your present beliefs and perceptions may open up many new dimensions to living. Develop a presence of mind to question everything you believe. Learn to weed out old, unworkable beliefs. At the same time, develop the ability to adopt new values and fresh behaviors to see whether they are workable.

Flat-Earth Thinkers On A Round World

> *"The fact that an opinion has been widely held is no evidence whatever that it is not entirely absurd; indeed in view of the silliness of the majority of mankind, a widespread belief is more likely to be foolish than sensible."*
>
> *- Bertrand Russell*

Your ability to enjoy leisure time will be determined by how much you have been able to avoid being brainwashed by mainstream society. All societies try to impose morals and values on their members. As we can see from history, these morals and values are often detrimental to many individuals.

Note that I am saying society tries to do this; society does not succeed with everyone. Not all members subscribe to the general values and morals prevalent in a particular society. There are some people who pay attention. Individuals with a presence of mind about the world will not be influenced by society's wishes, if they see what society believes is suspect. These are the people who lay the groundwork for society to progressively change for the better.

Several centuries ago, despite evidence to the contrary, mainstream society still went on believing the earth was flat. The belief in a flat world was not easily surrendered.

Holding on to outmoded beliefs is as prevalent today as it was several centuries ago. People don't want to give up a belief which they have held for a long time. They hate to admit their belief was wrong, this being a blow to their egos. Belief becomes an incurable disease. Rather than subscribe to a new and different viewpoint, which may be beneficial to them, people go on hanging to the old.

> *"If you see in any given situation only what everybody else can see, you can be said to be as much a representative of your culture that you are a victim of it."*
>
> *- S. I. Hayakawa*

North American society, like most societies before it, thinks it is as progressive as it can be. However, our society is no different from many societies before it; it is infiltrated by many flat-earth thinkers. When it comes to work and leisure, many of our society's values and morals are outdated. Future societies may look at today's common beliefs about work and leisure as primitive, much as we look at the old belief, that the world was flat, as primitive.

3. The Morality Of Work Is The Morality Of Slaves

Thinking About Work

If you want to enhance the quality of your spare time, challenging your thinking about work and leisure is a good place to start. As you put some old ideas about work to sleep, you will come into your own as a person. No matter what your situation in life, you will find more enjoyment just from being able to have a more positive perspective about yourself and the quality of your life.

> Work: The thing that interferes with golf."
>
> - Frank Dane

Exercise #3-1- Something To Think About

As stated in Chapter 2, your ability to enjoy leisure time will in part depend on how flexible you are in your views. To give some thought to your values and attitudes about work, answer the following questions:

Do you believe that hard work is the key to success in this world? Why?

Do you think that it is best for our society to have every able person from 16 years old to 65 years old gainfully employed at least 40 hours a week?

Are modern-day unemployed panhandlers a drain on society?

There are no right answers to the above questions. This chapter is meant to challenge your morals and values surrounding work and leisure. I am hoping the following content will stimulate your thinking in directions other than you might normally take.

The Protestant Work Ethic Ruined A Good Thing

Your resume says you're incredibly lazy, and won't take a job if your life depends on it.

That's absolutely correct!

PERSONNEL

Let's go back in history to a time when people looked at work in a different light. Greeks in an earlier era thought work was vulgar. Work, just for the sake of work, signified slavery and nonproductivity. The only reason for work was to acquire more leisure.

Leisure was not just a rest from work; it was desirable as an end in itself. As should be the case, leisure time was the most productive time. One could use this time to think, learn and self-actualize. Considering there is no greater goal strived for by sophisticated people than to grow and become self-actualized, ancient Greeks seemed to have their thinking in order.

Then along came the Protestant work ethic to ruin this perfectly intelligent way to think about work. For some strange reason, society took a wrong turn and adopted the new work ethic. This reversed the roles for work and leisure. Work became the productive activity. Leisure was to be used only for allowing individuals to rest, so they could be more effective in the workplace.

This "modern" mode of thinking developed to a point where it

28

relies on guilt to make it more effective. Guilt, in a perverse way, works to nullify the pleasure experience. The negative emotions are so strong for many people that feelings of guilt surface when they go on vacations. Unable to enjoy their time off, these bubbleheads come back from their vacations having attained negative emotional benefits.

> *"The best test of the quality of a civilization is the quality of its leisure."*
>
> *- Irwin Edman*

This is the North American way: The majority view work with such respect that they boast how many hours a day they work. Even if the job is routine and tiresome, and the financial gain is nothing from working overtime, they can't resist letting people know how hard they have been working. They have become martyrs, giving up the opportunity for self-actualization in return for the privilege of slaving, which primarily benefits the company rather than themselves.

Since the reversal in the roles of work and leisure, work has become the sole organizing principle and means for self-expression. In the modern world, leisure has a much lower status than work. To many people, leisure represents idleness and a waste of valuable time. Without work, many people exhibit a deterioration in their personalities and a loss in self-esteem. New faults such as drinking and unfaithfulness appear in many individuals when they lose their jobs.

Modern technology in Western societies has made it possible for leisure to be a privilege, not only for aristocrats, but one distributed to many different people in the community. I am sure the progressive philosophers in ancient Greece would be greatly confused to learn many people in the modern world, having more leisure than ever before, are not quite sure what to do with their extra time. They would be most perplexed by today's individuals, who work long hours, even though they are financially well-off.

> *"There is a no more fatal blunderer than he who consumes the greater part of his life getting his living."*
>
> *- Henry David Thoreau*

I am not quite sure what has caused society to accept the reversal in the roles of work and leisure, and the effects of such a reversal. There is one thing I am sure about: The ancient Greeks would not only be confused, but disgusted with the progress in humankind. To them, it would appear many people in modern day American society have developed masochistic tendencies.

Don't Work Because It's Moral To Do So

Working at an unpleasant job when it is necessary for one's survival is rational. Working at an unpleasant job, when one is financially well-off and doesn't have to work, is irrational. Nevertheless, many well-off people toil away at unpleasant jobs, because they believe it is moral to be working.

> *"Don't be too moral. You may cheat yourself out of life so."*
>
> *- Henry David Thoreau*

Most people have not stopped to consider that a great deal of harm may result from the belief that work is a virtue. Although it is necessary for our survival, work does not contribute as much to individual well-being as many think it does.

Just to set things straight, I am not saying that we should avoid as much work as possible. You may have erroneously assumed I suffer from the fear of work (which is called ergophobia by psychologists). On the contrary, I still get a great deal of satisfaction from most work I choose to do. Writing this book is one example.

My point is that working for the sake of working can be detrimental to our well-being and enjoyment in life. This is by no means a new relevation. Bertrand Russell, a little while ago, stated that North America's attitude toward work and leisure was outdated, and contributed to the misery in society. In his essay, *In Praise Of Idleness*, Russell stated:

"The morality of work is the morality of slaves, and the modern world has no need of slavery."

> *"Let us be grateful to Adam: he cut us out of the blessing of idleness and won for us the curse of labor."*
>
> *- Mark Twain*

I would like to have you believe that Bertrand borrowed this line from me, but this would sound far fetched, considering he wrote this in 1932, almost 60 years ago. Reading Russell's essay today is eye opening due to its relevance in this day and age. It is interesting to see how little our values have changed in 60 years, although our world has dramatically changed. Old values and beliefs are hard to surrender.

Let us use an example to illustrate the ludicrous results which can occur from hanging on to the belief hard work is a virtue. Suppose at any given moment the world needs X number of paper clips for its operations. With conventional technology, Y number of people are needed to produce these paper clips. They all work ten hours a day and everyone wishes they had more leisure time. Suppose someone invents a new and more efficient machine for making paper clips. Now, only half as many people as before are required to produce X number of paper clips. In a sensible world, the paper-clip makers would all work half as many hours as they worked before. They would all have much more leisure time.

The world is not this sensible. Because people still hang on to the belief that they should all work ten hours a day, all paper-clip makers work these hours until there is a surplus in paper clips. Eventually, half of the workers are laid off. This guarantees everyone is miserable. The laid-off workers have too much leisure time, and not enough money. The retained workers are overworked, and have too little leisure.

Instead of contributing to everyone's happiness, the unavoidable increase in leisure adds to everyone's misery. The morality of work ends up contributing to major unhappiness. Only by having our morals change, to keep pace with our changing world, can we avoid these unhealthy situations.

The Law Of Detrimental Returns

Hard work is supposed to be the key to success. Contrary to public belief, this is seldom the case. For some mysterious reason, people, who espouse the virtues of hard work in our society, overlook the fact that several million people keep their noses to the grindstone throughout their careers, and wind up with nothing but flat noses. They certainly don't fulfill their dreams.

Because a certain amount of work is good for us, it doesn't automatically follow that twice as much work should be twice as

All keeping my nose to the grindstone for 25 years has given me is a sore nose.

good for us. The law of diminishing returns takes over after a certain point. We gain less and less for each extra hour that we work.

Things go from bad to worse. After the point of diminishing returns, we can reach another point. This is where we reach what I call the law of detrimental returns. This means any extra work after this level will actually subtract from our overall enjoyment in life. Additional time spent at work contributes to many undesirable consequences associated with mental and physical ailments. One such ailment in the 1980's and 1990's is chronic fatigue syndrome. This ailment is also known as yuppie disease.

A Nation Gone Mad With The Work Ethic

Japanese Poster Promoting Leisure

Can you imagine this? Everyone in the nation loves working more than anything else. The work ethic gets so out of hand that factory workers, even though they are entitled to only seven days annual vacation, routinely refuse to take their entire vacations, preferring instead to stay at the plant and work.

The whole nation has gone mad. Business people, like everyone else, still insist on working six days a week. Although they are entitled to 20 days vacation, they take no more than factory workers. When business people take vacations, they don't know how to relax. Instead, they behave like maniacs, rushing back and forth, exhausting themselves trying to get in as much leisure as possible. The problem is they are so brainwashed with the work ethic that they don't quite know what leisure is. Things get so bad that health in the nation starts to suffer. The government eventually steps in with programs to teach people how to have more leisure.

Imagine the Ministry of Labor in the United States or Canada promoting taking it easy through more leisure. This would be severly criticized in either country. However, the situation described above is real; it is one happening in Japan.

The Japanese government, with its long term focus, has made one of its objectives the improvement of the quality of life through more leisure. Through its Ministry of Labor, it has a poster series promoting more time off for workers. One such poster says, "Let's realize a five-day work-week society." The Ministry also publishes a handbook giving workers ideas on how to take time off under the title, *Try Your Best: Salaryman's Guide to Relaxation.*

Nearly two thirds of Japanese people taking part in a survey said they take less than ten vacation days a year. However, many workers would like more time off. Guess what most wanted to do with more leisure? More than 85 percent just wanted to sleep more. One would have to surmise either they are extremely tired from overwork, or the work ethic has made them a very boring society.

Hard Work Is A Killer

Many Japanese are not only tired, but exhausted, from overwork. A survey conducted by the Fukoku Life Insurance Company of Japan reported nearly one half of Japan's salaried employees fear that their jobs will drive them to an early death.

> *"Death is nature's way of telling us to slow down."*
>
> *- Graffiti in washroom*

Japan's work ethic is so strong that they have even developed a disease to go along with it. "Karoshi" is the Japanese term for sudden death from overwork. Reports indicate ten percent of male fatalities are attributed to overwork. Families are now successfully suing companies for contributing to the deaths of loved ones.

Personally, I feel individuals, whether Japanese, American, or Canadian, who die from overwork, have no one to blame but themselves. Anyone crazy enough to work that hard, when there are so many wonderful things to do in life, will get little sympathy from me.

Furthermore, I don't know why Japan had to come up with another term for this disease. They already had one; the term Hari Kari would have done nicely.

Bart Simpson's Philosophy Brings Hope

The Simpsons motivate me a lot more than Dale Carnegie ever did.

Like young American adults, young Japanese adults are showing more sanity than their elders when it comes to the work ethic. Values are changing for the better in both nations.

A reflection of the changing values can be seen on Japan's hottest TV program in the early 1990's. Chibi Marukochan, Japan's version of Bart Simpson, is a girl who has been getting top TV billing all over the nation. She has charmed children and adults alike, especially adult women between 20 and 25. Two in five TV sets tune to this Sunday cartoon showing Chibi as a relentless mediocre third grader, who growls and avoids work as much as possible.

The work ethic is now being seen as a sham by many young adults in Japan. They are even more likely than American youth to question dedication to work. The new generation, or "shinjinrui", also have little interest in dedicating themselves to working for only one company, as their parents have. Younger Japanese adults, like their American counterparts, not only would like a more intelligent lifestyle, they are demanding it.

Loafing Is For High Achievers

"It is better to have loafed and lost than never to have loafed at all."

- James Thurber

Many great achievers in the history of humankind have been lazy according to their society's standards. Although it sounds like a contradiction, great achievers spent time in great measure avoiding work. They weren't necessarily lazy, but the majority in society, probably somewhat due to envy, viewed them as such.

Being creative loafers, these achievers spent considerable time relaxing and thinking. A creative loafer is one who accomplishes something significant but does not overdo it with sustained activity. Creative loafing results in relaxed, but productive activity.

Although they didn't work long hours, many achievers through the ages were highly efficient and productive when they worked on their imaginative and valuable projects. Of course, because they took time to loaf, they were more relaxed, happier, and healthier than they would have been if they had overworked themselves.

Why Panhandlers Contribute To Society

One day, I emphatically stated to a friend that I often contribute to charities, but I won't give money to panhandlers. I let her know panhandlers are lazy degenerates who serve no purpose, except to harass me while I am walking down the street on my merry way to a favorite bistro.

This friend quickly gave me a lesson in one of my seminar topics: the ability to be flexible in one's thinking. Someone once said we teach best those things we need to know; there may be some truth to this.

I always wanted to be a degenerate panhandler, but I couldn't quite make it. That's why I got myself an office job.

I was informed by my friend that panhandlers, because of their lifestyle, utilize few resources and are not a drain on the environment as are working people. Panhandlers don't steal for their money but ask for it. They make certain givers happy by giving them the opportunity to help someone. Also in a world where full employment becomes less likely with time, every panhandler not working in the system means one less person competing for a valuable job.

As I reflected upon this, it occurred to me that some working people whom I know are more degenerate, and don't make as many contributions to society. I no longer get upset when I encounter panhandlers. Occasionally, I give them money and think about their great contributions to society. Other times, I beat them to the punch and ask them for money first. In this way, I may be able to make the same contributions to society as they make.

35

To Be A Yuppie Is To Be A Successful Failure

I used to be a successful yuppie, but I gave up my nervous twitches, paste-on smile, and therapist, and it ruined my career.

There are two things phonier than a three-dollar bill: One is a tree filled with elephants; the other is a successful yuppie. During the 1980's, and into the early 1990's, yuppies, with their paste-on smiles and masks of false happiness, have lived halloween 365 days a year.

Yuppies, in their madness, made the work ethic trendy. With hard work was supposed to come incredible success, and the good life from excess materialism. Being a yuppie means it is easier and better to be recognized for what one owns, rather than for whom one is.

The world yuppies inhabited, and to which many others aspire, isn't all it's wrapped up to be. Due to their wealth-warped mentalities, and addictions to overwork, yuppies in great numbers suffer from hypertension, ulcers, heart disease, alcohol abuse, and drug dependence. To cope with this, many yuppies, some also to keep up with the latest trends, are seeing therapists. There are specialist therapists for lawyers, specialist therapists for doctors, and even specialist therapists for yuppie therapists.

When it comes to leisure time, North American yuppies are not much better off than the Japanese. Despite their abundant salaries, yuppies find leisure time the hardest thing to buy. According to a Harris survey, the amount of leisure time enjoyed by the average American shrunk 37 percent since 1973. Yuppies, with their long work days, had their spare time shrink even more than the average. For many of these young urban professionals, life has become so harried that even leisure is done according to schedule, if it is fitted in at all.

Many children in yuppie families have missed their childhood, because their parents are too busy chasing whatever they are chasing. Some yuppies arrange to meet their children sometime during the week by making appointments with them. Other yuppies are training their children from an early age to be "successful" like them. Their childrens' schedules are so filled up with activities that they don't know what it is like to just relax, and "do nothing."

> *"No man who is in a hurry is quite civilized."*
>
> *- Wilf Durant*

In light of all these complications, people who chose a yuppie lifestyle, and are still trying to maintain it at all costs, certainly don't appear to be rational people brimming over with sensible thoughts. Although they boast about how hard they work, they don't appear to have many overworked brain cells. Pamela Ennis, an industrial psychologist based in Toronto, who has counselled many yuppies laid off in the early 1990's, was quoted in *Report On Business* magazine: "This generation has a screw loose. They don't understand that a condo in Collingwood or a BMW is not going to bring them satisfaction."

The success that yuppies strive for is self-defeating. Considering all their attendant problems, we should have more appropriately called them yuffies (young urban failures), rather than yuppies.

Is Your Life All About Stuff?

As ridiculous as it seems, our primary purpose in life is to acquire material goods using the monetary fruits we receive from our work. Yuppies have undertaken this purpose to the extreme. The rest of us are not much better; we have not stopped to think about our real purpose in life.

> *"All my possessions for a moment of time."*
>
> *- Queen Elizabeth I, 1603*

George Carlin's comedy act about stuff says a lot. I don't recall how he exactly says it, but it goes something like this:

Right from the time we are young we are given stuff. We learn to like stuff. As we grow up, we want even more stuff. We continually ask our parents for money so we can buy stuff.

Then when we are of age, we get a job to buy stuff. We get a house in which we put our stuff. Needless to say, we must buy a car to haul our stuff around. Because we soon get too much stuff, our house becomes too small. So we get a bigger house. Now we don't have enough stuff for the big house, so we buy more stuff. We need a new car because we have worn our old car out carrying this stuff around. And on it goes. We never get around to having all the stuff we want.

All this stuff about stuff is funny, but at the same time dismaying. It shows how our addiction to working supports our addiction to getting more and more stuff, much of which we definitely don't need.

What The "G" in GNP Really Stands For

> *"If all economists were laid end to end, they would not reach a conclusion."*
>
> *- George Bernard Shaw*

Economists, people in business, and politicians tell us we will all be better off if our countries have substantial increases in the gross national product (GNP). Gross national product is the value of all services and products sold in a country during any given year. It is the measurement that tells us if we have been successful as a nation. The wise men and women of business and economics tell us that the goal in any country's economy is growth in GNP.

Another goal for the economy is to have no unemployment. The ability to generate new jobs is dependent on economic growth. A certain level of GNP is supposed to provide jobs for everyone able to work, whether they want to or not.

Having taught economics courses at educational institutions, I have always had a problem with GNP as a yardstick for how well a country is doing. GNP is improved by increases in such questionable activities as consumption of cigarettes and the production of military equipment. A substantial increase in car accidents will favorably affect GNP because more funerals, hospital visits, car repairs, and new car purchases will result.

> *"If all economists were laid end to end, it would not be a bad idea."*
>
> *- Anon*

With the growth in GNP considered such an important yardstick, it surprises me that the skipper on Exxon's Valdez didn't receive a Nobel prize for economics. The gross national product in the United States increased by $1.7 billion due to the

Exxon oil spill. More drunken skippers working with reckless abandon would do wonders for the GNP by generating many more massive oil spills. More people would also be employed.

Growth in GNP for the sake of growth doesn't necessarily reflect something good for society. It should be pointed out that growth for the sake of growth is also the philosophy of cancer cells. Instead of standing for the gross national product, GNP should stand for the grossness of the national product.

The True Measure of A Nation's Success

Recently I talked to a couple who had traveled extensively. They were fortunate to meet the King of Bhutan. As a country, Bhutan is relatively undeveloped. The people are poor, but not poverty stricken. Nevertheless, the people in the country are content with their state in life.

> *"Much happiness is lost in the pursuit of it."*
>
> *- Anon*

When the couple asked about Bhutan's low gross national product, the King replied, "We don't believe in gross national product; we believe in gross national happiness."

So how about this folks? Let's use gross national happiness (GNH) rather than GNP to measure how well the countries of the world are doing. We can probably create a more workable world. There is something we must do first: We must find out how to eliminate all the economists.

Taking It Easy For The Environment

Caring for the environment has become a topic of paramount importance. Yet few people are willing to admit that their own wealth-warped values and excessive drive for success contribute to serious environmental pollution. If they were to take it easy and work less, they would help create a greener world.

Practically all work involves altering matter at or near the earth's surface relative to other matter. This is dependent upon the utilization of natural resources. Any use of natural resources contributes to pollution in our environment. Most increases in GNP are at a substantial cost to our environment.

> *"Try not to be a person of success, but rather a person of virtue."*
>
> *- Albert Einstein*

Imperative to a greener planet is a reduction in our use of natural resources. We in North America can probably get by with half the resources which we use, and still maintain a good standard of living. This can be accomplished, in part, by changing our values. What we must do is eliminate frivilous work and consumption, such as the production of stupid trinkets and gadgets, which people buy and use for a week or two before throwing them away.

Robert Paehlke, author of *Environmentalism & the Future of Progressive Politics,* is much more eloquent than I can be in stating these points. Here is an exerpt from his interview with Don Alexander for the July/August, 1990 issue of *Alternative Magazine:*

"The cure for every ill is definitely not a product. We don't need instant food, video games, diet coke, macho cars, or for that matter, so many copies of newspapers as fat as the *Toronto Star* or the *New York Sunday Times,* whether on recycled paper or not. .... these purchases are not compulsory.

How does one "challenge" these realities? All one can say is that many, if not most, of the products of North American industrial society are unnecessary and that all production of goods contributes in part to the ecological damage we inflict. The best "eco-shopping" guide is the suggestion to stay home and read a library book, or to go for a long walk away from, rather than to, the shopping mall ..... "

Saving our planet will require more than recycling bottles and cans. There is something ridiculous about producing unnecessary trinkets and various other products, just for keeping people busy working at jobs. It is apparent that individuals, who are able to take it easy, work less, and consume less, are making an important contribution to a greener world.

Towards Less Work And Better Living

The work ethic may be doing us more harm than good. We have to change our work-focused and wealth-warped mentalities if we are to have a better sense of what is important for our happiness. Studs Terkel in his book, *Working*, stated that the time has come to revise the work ethic. Many modern North American beliefs contribute to people being slaves, when they don't have to be. The concept of work, as we know it, is long overdue for review.

The modest values from the 18th century are more appropiate for today than the 20th-century values we have adopted. The problem is we lost the sense of enough in the 1980's. Most of us cherished the Robert Campeau and Donald Trump values of habitual striving for more and bigger stuff. For the 1990's and beyond, instead of the Campeau and Trump style, the profile of the 18th-century gentleman, who made his modest amount of money and then retired to more worthwhile pursuits, makes greater sense. An inner world of personal growth, replacing the external world of materialistic growth, will contribute to greater satisfaction and well-being.

Now that I have a big pile of money, I'm still not self-actualized. Maybe I need a bigger pile.

Less emphasis on the need to be working and the obsession with stuff is in order. Working is necessary, but not to the degree most people think. Introducing more modest materialistic goals will do wonders for our environment, and give us the opportunity to enjoy a more leisurely lifestyle.

41

The Real Stuff Of Life

The comments in the previous sections point out a few shortcomings of the values common to North American society. If you have adopted these values, you may want to consider seeing things differently. Having strict beliefs, that work is virtuous and play is frivilous, will impair your ability to respond to periods of unemployment and retirement. If you are working, these same values may leave you unfulfilled, due to an imbalance in your lifestyle.

Being a flexible thinker will allow you to see that modifying your values to have a more modest emphasis on working and materialism has its merits. Less work in your life can have many payoffs. Time away from the workplace, no matter what your situation, can be an opportunity to learn in new ways, and grow as a person.

Someone who works long hours and owns many gadgets, trinkets, and other "stuff" is not a better person than the individual who works fewer hours and owns less. The addiction to stuff tends to alienate us from other people and the environment.

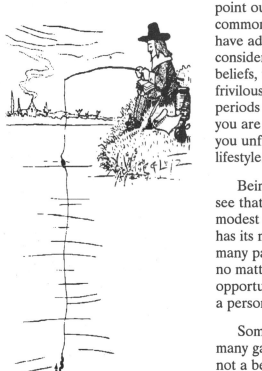

That man up there isn't really fishing. He just caught me and threw me back in. I think he's some weirdo scientist trying to see if worms enjoy scuba diving.

In the higher order in life, stuff around us - cars, houses, stereos, jobs - they're facilities and nothing else. They are not the source of our happiness. The things we own, the places we live, and the jobs we have are secondary in importance. True success shouldn't be measured by what we own or what we do for a living. Our real essence is of a higher order. The only things that should matter in the end relate to how well did we live: what did we learn, how much did we laugh and play, and how much did we love. This is the real stuff of life!

42

4. Working Less Just For The Health Of It

The Trap With No Cheese

If we took a rat and consistently put cheese in the third of several tunnels, the rat would eventually figure out the cheese is always in the third tunnel. The rat would go directly to the third tunnel without looking in the other tunnels. However, if we one day started putting the cheese in the sixth tunnel, the rat would keep on going to the third tunnel only for so long. Sooner or later the rat would realize there is no cheese in the third tunnel, and start looking in the other tunnels. It would discover the cheese is now in the sixth tunnel. The rat would now consistently show up in the tunnel with the cheese.

The difference between a rat and the majority in society is the majority will remain in a tunnel, when it is obvious there is no cheese in it. Going after the cheese, most human beings get themselves into a trap from which they never escape. It's pretty hard to get the cheese, when one is caught in a trap that has no cheese left, and in some cases had no cheese in it in the first place.

> *"I don't want the cheese, I just want to get out of the trap."*
>
> *- Spanish Proverb*

Cheese here represents happiness, satisfaction, and fulfillment. Today unhappiness in great measure exists in the ranks of most management circles. This is a contention by Jan Halper, a Palo Alto psychologist and management consultant, who spent ten years exploring the careers and emotions of over 4000 male executives. Halper found many men in management appeared to be happy, but were just the opposite. Of those in middle management, 58 percent felt they had wasted many years in their lives while struggling to achieve their goals. They were bitter about the many sacrifices they made during these years. These men were not doing what they should have been doing to have a balanced life. Other research shows up to 70 percent of white-collar workers are unhappy with their jobs. The irony is that a majority of white-collar workers are dissatisfied with what they are doing, but they are spending more and more time doing it.

> *"There is more to life than increasing its speed."*
>
> *- Mahatma Gandhi*

We use the term "being in the rat race", but it isn't an appropriate one; it is demeaning to rats. Rats won't stay in a tunnel without cheese. It would be more appropriate for rats to use the term "being in the human race", when they find themselves doing ridiculous things like going down the same tunnel without finding any cheese.

Reading more material from this chapter isn't necessary if you are a rat, or if you are a mentally and financially prosperous human being in a position where you aren't working, and don't intend to for the rest of your life. However, this chapter may be valuable to you if you are still working at a job, or if you are unemployed and plan to go back to work sometime in the future. Jobs don't always provide all the different types of cheese for which people are looking. With tunnel vision and ignorance being two big hindrances to human beings attaining satisfaction and fulfillment in their lives, the content in this chapter is intended to help you avoid the traps that appear in many jobs. It is also designed to help put some balance in your life, and prepare you for the time when you retire from work.

Do You Know Who You Are?

In helping you get a proper perspective on who you are and whether you are a workaholic, here is simple exercise for you to do:

Exercise #4-1 - A Simple Question?

Take a few moments in answering this simple question:

Who are you?

In doing the above exercise, practically all working people will write down what they do for a living, along with some other things such as what nationality they are, what religion they follow, whether they are married, where they live, and how old they are. The point is that what people do for a living is the thing on which most people focus. Few people associate interests away from the job as part of their identity. This reveals that most people's identities are tied to their jobs.

> *"One of the symptoms of an approaching nervous breakdown is the belief that one's work is terribly important."*
>
> *- Bertrand Russell*

In today's generation, managers have invested a lot emotionally and financially in their careers. Their sense of identity comes from their skills and talents. Corporate America has been telling us we get to build our character by working and doing things "productive" in organizations. We have learned to define ourselves by our jobs. There is something seriously wrong with this: If we think we are what we do for a living, we have lost most of our character.

How much of your identity is tied to your job? If you are a lawyer who has become so immersed in your job that all your identity is tied to it, you will answer that you are a lawyer in response to "Who are you?" That is exactly what all other lawyers who tie most of their identity to their jobs will say in answer to this question. Your identity of "a lawyer" will sound the same as all other lawyers who respond with the same answer. If your identity is mainly tied to your job, you may be limiting yourself as a person. Unless you love your job so much that you are totally blown away by it, your job should comprise only a minute part of your identity.

Yes, this job will definitely enhance my identity. If I get it, my BMW won't be repossessed.

When you put all your life into a job, there is the danger it will chip away at your personality until there is nothing left. "A lawyer" or any other occupation should not be who you are. An occupation is what you do to earn money. Who you are should be your essence. Your essence is your character and your individuality. It is those qualities that make you different from other people.

To find out who you are, look inside yourself for your own decisions, tastes, and interests. Don't let work become the only thing with meaning. Ensure that you develop hobbies and interests aside from work, that have just as much or more meaning than your job. Your self-image will then be something other than just your job. Listen to the intuitive voices within yourself, and not the logical voices in your organization, the establishment, or society. The best place to display your uniqueness is in your personal life away from work. When you are asked who you are, most of your identity should be associated with your essence, which you display in pursuing personal interests in your leisure time.

Ignorance Runs Rampant In Today's Corporate World

In today's world, outmoded attitudes and values possessed by many corporate executives help to perpetuate a work environment characterized by workaholism. This is damaging employees' health. Ignorance, at all levels including the higher echelons in management, runs rampant in major corporations across North America. Comfortable in this sea of ignorance, workaholics are not only tolerated, but respected. Because workaholism is about greed and power, many business leaders love workaholics. In many departments, where in numerous cases most workers can be classified as workaholics, it's fashionable to put in 60 to 80 hours a week. It's also fashionable to be in a hurry and overextended in one's work. Some managers even feel heroic to be overcommitted all the time.

> *"Ignorance is never out of style. It was in fashion yesterday, it is the rage today, and it will set the pace tomorrow."*
>
> *- Frank Dane*

This condition has serious implications: Workaholics are no different from any other addicts. All addicts are neurotics with a serious problem. Workaholics, like alcoholics, are in a state of denial about the existence of a problem but suffer from the serious consequences arising from the addiction. The same is true with people who support addicts; they are no better than addicts, neurotics at best.

Why do corporations support addiction? Anne Wilson Schaef explains this in great detail in her book, *When Society Becomes An Addict.* She states that addictive behavior is the norm in American society. Society itself functions as an addict, as do a lot of organizations. In her later book, *The Addictive Organization,* Schaef and her co-author, Diane Fassel, go into great detail about why most large organizations are affected by addictions, and themselves function like addictive individuals.

To serve their own interests, corporations have encouraged and promoted workaholism. Under the guise of quality and excellence, the corporate work ethic puts the corporation ahead of everything else. The company's success means it shouldn't matter if an individual's physical or mental health is wiped out, or if his or her marriage is ruined.

Promoting the importance of work and emphasizing the need to be in a hurry go hand in hand with promoting productivity. In reality, this only appears to promote productivity. Having company employees work longer, harder, and faster, while sacrificing their leisure time, doesn't necessarily mean more will be accomplished in the organization. In fact, the result can be quite the contrary. Less will be accomplished in the long run, because productivity and efficiency will sooner or later suffer from the decreased effectiveness of workers suffering from stress and burnout. It is interesting that strong-willed individuals are more likely to burn out than so-called wimps, because the strength possessed by the strong-willed is based on denial.

> *"He worked like hell in the country so he could live in the city, where he worked like hell so he could live in the country."*
>
> *- Don Marquis*

Careless mistakes and employees with no time to think can make the organization less innovative and less productive in the long run. Contrary to popular belief, always being in a hurry to get something done is not productive. A frantic routine leaves no time for thinking. Creativity will not flow if not enough time is made available for it. An ability to sit back, ponder the big picture, and take the long-term view represents a productive and successful worker.

> *"By working faithfully eight hours a day you may eventually get to be a boss and work twelve hours a day."*
>
> *- Robert Frost*

The consequences from the mad world in corporate life are far reaching. In the frenzy of working hard and day-to-day survival, many people have lost their personal dreams, and zest for living. Deprived family and social lives are the results of overwork and stress. For those feeling burnout, there is no more purpose, meaning, and vigor in living.

If we look back in time to ancient Greece, the modern workaholic yuppie seems like another case of history (along with ignorance) repeating itself. Plato in early Greece criticized those people ignorant and foolhardy enough to evade leisure by working too much. He warned them about getting caught up in luxury, power, reputation, influence, and excessive amusements. Work as the center of existence was to be avoided. Plato felt people, who kept working after they had met their basic needs, were missing out on more important pursuits.

Go To Jail And Live Longer

Your high-stress job may do you more harm than you ever imagined. It may even make you stupid. A recent research study led researchers to conclude prolonged exposure to stress can speed up the aging in brain cells and interfere with learning and memory. Long-term intelligence may actually be decreased with the damage to brain cells from the effects of stress.

If you would like to escape stress common to the modern work world, and increase your health and longevity at the same time, try robbing a bank or two. Make sure you get caught in the act. Jail may be the best place where you can escape stress. Researchers at the Institute Bustave Roussy in Villejuif, France have discovered that French prisoners live longer and have lower rates of disease, including cancer and heart disease, than other Frenchmen. The longer they stayed in jail, the lower was their death rate. Why? It certainly has nothing to do with the use of alcohol, cigarettes, or drugs which are used by most prisoners. The researchers postulate that prison life is simply less stressful than normal life. Prisoners have a more leisurely lifestyle than the general population.

These prisoners are onto something. They have found a way to escape work and get more leisure in their lives. You may want to commit some crime, get caught at it, and go to jail. More leisure will improve your health and increase your longevity. Of course, going to jail is not the only way to attain more leisure in your life.

Crazy George Is Not That Crazy

Most work in which people engage is routine and tiresome. Millions in North America want to flee from their jobs but can't figure out where to flee. These people should talk to my friend whom some of us call Crazy George. He may be a great role model. We call George "crazy" because he is different. One different thing about George is he does not like working for organizations. He considers it demeaning to his character. Having others tell him what to do, how to do it, and what time to come to work are not things George relishes. There are many other characteristics of the typical workplace which George despises.

Living on the fringes, he does a little work here and there. Crazy George is seldom in a rush. He has been a third-year-apprentice carpenter for something like 14 years and never seems to last on any one job for more than a month or two. He also does some freelance auto-body work. His income is often below the poverty line; however, due to his spending money only on the basics, George has managed to put away more money in the bank than is saved by many people who make $75,000 or more a year.

The interesting thing about Crazy George is he is 48 years old and looks like he is 38. On the other hand, I know "successful" working people who are 48 years old and look like they are 58. George looks much younger than he is because his lifestyle is very healthy. Like the French prisoners, he does not have to contend with the stresses with which the masses have to contend. If Crazy George maintains his condition, he will be able to work in his 80's if he has to. Because he has his freedom as well, Crazy George is even better off than the French prisoners. Considering all factors, I would say that Crazy George is not that crazy; the employed who indulge in excessive work are the crazy ones.

> *"I have never liked working. To me a job is an invasion of privacy."*
>
> *- Danny McGoorty*

49

Leisure Is In; Workaholism Is Passe

In the 1980's North Americans in the millions made work the center of their existence. In doing so, they distorted their lives and fell into emotional turmoil. The road to corporate success left many feeling hollow and shallow. Former dreams became today's nightmares. Many people realized they are slaves to their jobs and their possessions. Spending 50 to 80 hours a week at the workplace contributed to a loss of self. A total focusing on work destroyed what essence they once had. To make matters worse, job stress and burnout robbed them of their physical and mental well-being. They paid a big price for their involvement in voluntary slavery.

> *"America has become so tense and nervous it has been years since I've seen anyone sleep in church - and that is a sad situation."*
>
> *- Norman Vincent Peale*

The good news is that "the times, they are a-changing." As the world entered the 1990's, many employees started looking at work in a different light. For the first time in fifteen years, working Americans said leisure, rather than work, is the important thing in their lives. A total of 41 percent of respondents to the 1990 poll conducted by the Roper Organization chose leisure as the most important thing, while only 36 percent chose work as the most important. This is significant considering that in 1985 work came out ahead of leisure by a score of 46 percent to 33 percent. Many Canadians also don't value work above everything else in life. Out of approximately 15,000,000 individuals employed in Canada in 1988, 5,311,360 planned to take early retirement.

Evidence suggests more and more North Americans have a hunger for quiet and unhurried living. Refugees from stress and burnout are starting to leave organizations in droves. The 90's have become the decade for employees to try and get away from the madness at work, either by leaving work completely, or by adopting alternative work arrangements to create a better balance between work and leisure. Several newspapers have reported that the workaholic is passe. Leisure is in; free time is the ultimate status symbol for the 90's.

Even some organizations have seen the obvious; quality leisure in employees' lives contributes to the health of the organization. Many companies are discovering that healthy employees are happier and more productive. Considering that eighty percent of illness is related to lifestyle-related causes, it should be natural that companies would care about employees' increased health and morale gained from increased enjoyment in leisure activities. The result for the organization can be a tremendous payout in productivity, stamina, motivation, and good corporate image. Several major corporations have adopted training programs to promote wellness and a balanced lifestyle for their employees.

Organizations in the future will have no alternative. Employees will demand a better balance between work and leisure. *Fortune Magazine* in their August 27, 1990 issue reported on the changing values in corporate America. Unlike the baby boomers, today's recruits are not as likely to be workaholics lured by the trappings of money, title, security, and ladder climbing. They have a new attitude towards life and work. As should be, employees in their early twenties say leisure, lifestyle, and family are at least as important as work. Personally, I am happy about the change in values. I feel that this generation has more wholesome values than the baby boomers from my generation.

Leisure Lovers May Help Reduce Unemployment

The emphasis on quality in life and more leisure may in the long run benefit not only those having more leisure time. This may also benefit those having too much leisure and not enough work.

> *"We are always getting ready to live, but not really living."*
>
> *- Ralph Waldo Emerson*

A 1991 survey sponsored by Hilton Hotels Corporation surveyed employed people in the United States. The results indicated 48 percent of those responding would sacrifice a day's pay for an extra day off each week. More than 53 percent of employed women and 43 percent of working men are willing to forgo a day's pay for an extra day off. Another 17 percent of men and women would give a day's pay to get two days off per week. A similar survey recently conducted by the Conference Board of Canada indicated 35 percent of employed Canadians aged 25-44 would forego some of their salary for more time off.

With all the employed people wanting to work less for less pay, new possibilites are opened up for the unemployed. Frank Reid, a University of Toronto ecomomist, quoted in an article in *Western Living* magazine, stated 500,000 new jobs could be created in Canada by letting those who want to work less do so, and turning this extra work over to the unemployed. Correspondingly, in the United States, the number of new jobs created could be several million.

Unfortunately, organizational and societal rigidity towards adopting new employment options is creating barriers to opening up this opportunity for reducing unemployment. Hopefully these barriers will be removed in the near future. This will make many employed and many unemployed individuals happier due to a better balance in their lives.

To Be A Peak Performer, Work Less And Play More

> *"Work is the greatest thing in the world, so we should always save some of it for tomorrow."*
>
> *- Don Herold*

Reading a fiction thriller, working in the garden, or just daydreaming while lying in the hammock are ways to increase your productivity at work. If you want to be a peak performer at your job, try working less and playing more. A generous amount of leisure in your life will increase your wealth. I am talking about mental wealth. In the long run, you will likely also increase your financial wealth if you take more time for leisure.

Indulging in more leisure with side interests and hobbies has many benefits. One important benefit is hobbies and interests outside your employment help you to be more innovative in your job. While you are engaged in these other pursuits, your conscious mind takes a rest from your work-related problems. This allows your conscious mind to focus on things other than work. By developing interests and hobbies outside your field, you will keep your thinking fresh and in top condition. Your mind will be much more creative in generating those new ideas that contribute to your organization's innovativeness. Some of the most creative breakthroughs have been made when people's minds were off duty.

The average employed person is out of balance. This is true especially in business where many white-collar workers are working much more than a regular 40-hour work week. Those regularly working excessive hours are workaholics. Perfectionism, compulsiveness, and obsessiveness are traits which complement the workaholic mentality. It is important to realize workaholics are not peak performers - workaholics are weak performers. Workaholics are addicted to continually putting in long hours, and find no time for leisure. Considering the excessive work in which workaholics must indulge to get limited results, most are virtual incompetents. In fact, many workaholics end their careers by getting fired.

Because peak performers enjoy both work and play, they are more effective workers. Although they can turn on bursts of speed for a week or two, when needed, peak performers can be lazy (and proud of it) when the nature of the work is routine. The following comparisons point out the differences between workaholics and peak performers:

Workaholic	**Peak Performer**
⇨ Works long hours	⇨ Works regular hours
⇨ Has no defined goals - works to be active	⇨ Has defined goals - works towards a major objective.
⇨ Cannot delegate to others	⇨ Delegates as much as possible
⇨ No interests outside of work	⇨ Many interests outside of work
⇨ Misses vacations to work	⇨ Takes and enjoys vacations
⇨ Has shallow friendships developed at work	⇨ Has deep friendships developed outside of work
⇨ Always talks about work matters	⇨ Minimizes talk about work matters
⇨ Is always busy doing things	⇨ Can enjoy "goofing off"
⇨ Feels life is difficult	⇨ Feels life is a celebration

> *"Hard work is the soundest investment. It provides a neat security for your widow's next husband."*
>
> *- Anon*

Workaholism is a serious disease. If not treated in time, workaholism can result in mental and physical health problems. According to Barbara Killinger, author of the book, *Workaholics, The Respectable Addicts,* workaholics are emotional cripples. The tragedy is the work obsession of workaholics leads them to ulcers, back problems, insomnia, depression, heart attacks, and in many cases an early death.

If you are to be a peak performer, success in your life will not be confined to the office. Being a peak performer with a balanced lifestyle means your job is serving you rather than you are serving your job. Life/work planning consultants advocate a balanced lifestyle in which needs in six areas of life are satisfied. The six areas are: intellectual, physical, family, social, spiritual, and financial. Since many companies still deal with employees with the philosophy that security, pay, and retirement benefits are the only way to motivate them, there is a chance your job only adequately satisfies your needs in the financial and social areas. Your other four needs - family, intellectual, spiritual, and physical - then have to be satisfied away from work.

Figure #4-1 - Balancing Your Wheel Of Life

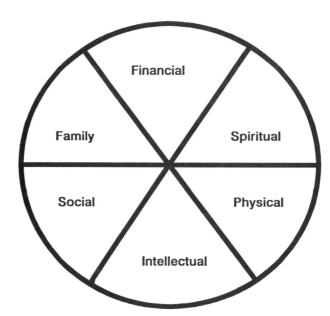

Leisureholics Have More Fun

By working diligently (sometimes not so diligently) for 40 years or more, many workers hope that one day they will cash in their chips for 15 to 20 years of fruitful leisure. Upon reaching retirement, many people are unprepared, because they have not pursued leisure while they were working. Most people don't change until they have to. They wait until retirement is a reality, and then desperately try to make the adjustment. For the unprepared, the adjustment at this time is extremely difficult due to the drastic change in circumstances. The time to start developing many interests and enjoying leisure is when one is working. A gradual adjustment is much easier to make.

In organizations, workers are being rewarded for structured thinking and tunnel vision which embody the corporate mission. If leisure activities are encouraged, most organizations encourage activities related to work, or those that will help employees perform work better. Most organizations are not interested in employees having many broad interests unrelated to work.

Another problem is many North Americans engage in leisure activities with little or no quality. The activities in which they engage are for the purpose of recuperating from a hectic day or week, and not for the sheer enjoyment from the activity. Many activities are not leisurely. Rather than relieve stress, the activities actually add to stress.

In the academic world, it is a case of publish or perish. In retirement, it can be a case of learn to handle leisure or perish. If you don't prepare yourself for your retirement, you will feel a tremendous sense of loss, as did George Eastman, the founder of Kodak, when he quit working (see quotation to the right). Your self-esteem will sink to the bottom of a rut where there is only futility and uselessness. Even if you don't do yourself in like George Eastman did, death can come rather early if you just sit around after you retire. Instead of enjoying the promised land of retirement, you will soon die of boredom, as many people do, and enter the real promised land (if you deserve to be there).

> *"My work is done, why wait?"*
>
> *- suicide note left by George Eastman, founder of Kodak*

It is in your best interests, especially if you want to eventually live the life of Riley, to have many and varied interests unrelated to your career. Leisure is not something to be saved up until you are totally without work. Living a balanced life means you will indulge in leisure throughout your whole life. If you are going to be addicted to anything, then be a leisureholic; leisureholics have more fun than workaholics.

As a leisureholic, not only will you have more fun, you will prepare yourself beforehand for the time when you could lose your job. Quality leisure done in a leisurely way, besides making you happier while working, prepares you for a better life when you retire, or find yourself unemployed. Pre-retirement consultants advocate employees start preparing and planning for their retirement when they are 35 years old or younger. Studies have shown that the sooner a pre-retirement course with leisure planning is undertaken, the greater the chance for attaining satisfaction and fulfillment in retirement. The reason is that interests and new skills not cultivated before retirement are difficult to cultivate after retirement.

Helen Thomas, United Press International bureau chief at the White House for over 25 years, states that of all past presidents she got to know - Johnson, Nixon, Carter, and Reagan - Jimmy Carter was the one who truly accepted retirement and found it satisfying (quoted from the book, *Are You Happy*, by Dennis Wholey). Jimmy Carter has been the most successful in retirement because his identity was not tied to the job, and to having to be recognized all the time. Carter also had many ongoing interests such as writing, working with wood, and building furniture, which he has actively pursued since leaving the presidency. The citizens of the United States appear to know Carter is the best off. In a recent poll, 45.1 percent of respondents named Carter as the living ex-president who conducted himself most effectiveley and appropriately since leaving office, while 18.5 percent chose Ronald Reagan, and 9 percent chose Richard Nixon.

Figure #4-2 - Before & After For A Workaholic

WORK RELATIONSHIP	~~WORK~~ RELATIONSHIP
Workaholic Before Retirement	*Workaholic After Retirement*

Figure #4-3 - Before & After For A Leisureholic

WORK RELATIONSHIP GOLF TENNIS JOGGING STAMP COLLECTING CHURCH READING GARDENING VOLUNTEERING FRIENDS *Leisureholic Before Retirement*	▬▬▬▬ RELATIONSHIP GOLF TENNIS JOGGING STAMP COLLECTING CHURCH READING GARDENING VOLUNTEERING FRIENDS *Leisureholic After Retirement*

Figure #4-2 shows the effect of losing a job when you have no interests. If you have only your job and a relationship (marriage or otherwise) to keep you busy, your life will be limited once you lose your job. Without a job, you are limited to your relationship for things to keep you active. Figure #4-3 shows the effect of losing your job if you have many interests and hobbies. As a leisureholic, you don't have to rely solely on your relationship for fulfillment, since you can shift your extra time to a range of activities and interests to keep you busy.

Breadth in interests is important. Life can feel empty if your interests aren't varied. While you are working, it is important to develop many eclectic interests outside of your career. Just one interest, such as golfing, will not be enough to fill your days. Ensure you have a varied combination, from writing books to playing golf to visiting friends to taking a course unrelated to your job. It is also important that you choose activities which provide some purpose and achievement.

> *"The first half of life consists of the capacity to enjoy without the chance; the last half consists of the chance without the capacity."*
>
> *- Mark Twain*

Leisure should be a quiet and enthusiastic absorption in things

After two weeks of vacation, you finally have a smile on your face.

I can't wait to get back in the office to tell everyone what a great time I had, even though I didn't.

done for the sake of themselves and unconnected to work in any way. When you take time for leisure, try and adopt the European approach rather than the American approach. There is an important contrast in the philosophy of leisure in America and Europe. In North America, corporate philosophy tends to rule employees' lives, even in leisure. Because America has a working tradition rather than a leisure tradition, leisure to corporate America has been a time for relief, and escape to recharge one's batteries for the work ahead. In Europe, leisure is viewed in a different light. Leisure is for leisure's sake and not for work's sake. The main purpose of vacations is for enjoying leisure, and not for recharging. Quality leisure in Europe is a result of a leisure-class tradition which has spanned many centuries.

For leisure to be effective during your career, it is best that leisure be done in a leisurely way, and not in an "unleisurely" way. The spirit in which you conduct your leisure time may actually make this time more stressful than work itself. In North America, the traditional vacation is more often than not another tightly scheduled week with an itinerary resembling a week at the office. The week is spent at a spa or ashram retreat with little or no choice for spontaneity. A ski holiday in the Rockies or the Alps is filled with so many activities that relaxation is nearly impossible. To add to the stresses, many vacationing employees keep in regular contact with the office. It is no wonder that the widely used Holmes and Rahe Social Readjustment Rating Scale for stress indicates people find vacations more stressful than they find the Christmas season, even though people experience quite a bit of stress before Christmas. Vacations would be much less stressful if people spent their time reading a book, getting to know the neighbors, or writing a novel just for the fun of it. More leisurely vacations are also better ways to prepare for retirement.

Another example of unleisurely leisure is one which I see at my tennis club. I go out and play tennis to get in shape and have fun. In contrast to this, many of the people on the tennis courts are even more competitive than they are in the corporate world. The looks on their faces indicate a level of seriousness normally reserved for funerals and wars. They will do anything to win, including pick the most talented partners, choose inferior opponents, or cheat at the game. If they don't win, they will lie to a friend about the result of the match. To me, these are not people enjoying leisure; these are people with serious problems.

To be leisurely, learn to take a rather unconventional approach to leisure. Don't be like the fast trackers in the corporate world who engage in their leisure with as much or more competitiveness than they show at the workplace; they miss the whole point behind leisure. Instead, take a vacation at home and refuse to keep in contact with the office. Take an unexpected day off to add some spontaneity to your life. When in between jobs, take a vacation for a month or two. The point is to be as leisurely as you can be. You will be more relaxed during your work life, and more prepared for your retirement.

> *"For fast acting relief, try slowing down."*
>
> *- Lily Tomlin*

Fire Yourself If Your Employer Doesn't

Work can unbalance your life. Some jobs demand unending attention and won't give you the opportunity to have a balanced lifestyle. The result is often an unhappy spouse, undisciplined kids, no social life, and a miserable you. If you're getting about as much payoff from your job as being the captain of the Titanic, then you must do something to change your state in life.

Here are some signals that your life is not in balance and you are probably in the wrong job:

- □ You take more than your share of mental-health days due to headaches, tension, and other stress-related complaints.
- □ You dread going to work practically every morning.
- □ You make field trips on the coldest days in winter even though your job is totally an office job.
- □ You just don't like this job because you can't

express your creative side.

- ☐ Your main interest in staying in this job is to cope for another 16 years before you can collect a good pension.
- ☐ The first hour of work is spent reading the boring sections of yesterday's newspaper.
- ☐ You are putting off routine things such as visiting friends, paying the bills, and returning phone calls.
- ☐ Because you're married to your job, your life is all work and no play.
- ☐ You long to be back in university or school even though you didn't like attending either one.
- ☐ About 5:00 o'clock on Sunday afternoons your stress level increases dramatically with thoughts that tomorrow you have to go back to work.
- ☐ You have nothing good to say about your company even though it recently made it to *The 100 Best Companies To Work For In America.*

We all have a tendency to grow comfortable with existing conditions, even those undesirable to us (there are many forms of mental illness). In the workplace we end up tolerating dead-end jobs, professions we dislike, and companies which mistreat us. The workplace can also be a major source of boredom. A Lou Harris survey found 40 percent of Americans are bored sick with their jobs. We resist making changes because we fear the unknown. I was one of these people at my engineering job. Reluctant to quit, I stayed on until I was fired. In retrospect, I now see that I subconsciously helped put on the shoe that kicked me out.

> *"Being a housewife and a mother is the biggest job in the world, but if it doesn't interest you, don't do it....... I would have made a terrible mother."*
>
> *- Katherine Hepburn*

The first day your job does not nourish and enthuse you is the day you should consider leaving. Fire yourself if your employer doesn't. Even if you generally like your job, but it takes more than 50 hours a week from your life and you are not pleased with your balance in life, it is time for action. If your spouse calls you a stranger, your kids are on drugs, and you are miserable - why not do something else? My advice is that you QUIT! Forget about these excuses: I can't quit because I need the security, I need to make payments on my big house, I want to send the

60

kids to college, and all the other excuses that arise. Don't wait for the right time. Do it now because there is never a right time; waiting for the right time is another convenient excuse to justify procrastination.

No matter how much money you earn, you will never be able to recover the 40 hours or more you are putting into a job that doesn't enliven you. It is impossible for you to buy back enough enjoyment in retirement to make up for what pleasure you missed while working at a lousy job. Ask yourself, "What good is the money going to do if I lose my health?" There are many rich people who can't buy their health back.

Many people work with the same company until retirement, even if they don't like their job or the company, because they don't want to give up their good salaries. Others, like two school teachers I know, hate what they are doing, but will not change careers because of the generous retirement benefits. Staying in an unpleasant job or undesirable career makes these people function at much less than an optimum level. It also increases their chances for experiencing burnout before retirement, so they don't get to enjoy the retirement benefits.

> *"When some fellers decide to retire, nobody knows the difference."*
>
> *- Kin Hubbard*

You are imprisoned by the system if you are working just for the money. Don't allow society's idea of financial security to dictate your life. Spending time at a job you hate, just to make money, will interfere with your ability to enjoy life. As odd as it seems, it will also interfere with your making money. There is a common feeling that getting one's financial state in order will help put the individual's other needs in place. The opposite is frequently true. Studies have confirmed that individuals, who satisfy their other needs first by doing what they like doing, generally end up making much more money than individuals who work just for the money in jobs they dislike. It is important to be growing in your job, doing what you like to do, and putting the talents to use that you want to put to use. Attitude jumps back into the picture; if you feel your work is valuable and enjoyable, chances are you will attract enough money to enjoy life.

It's not impossible to leave a job, just difficult. Don't fool yourself by thinking something is impossible, when it is only hard. If you want to do something and are committed to doing it, you can do it. There is a price to pay, but it will be worth it in the long run. Do your wife a favor, do your kids a favor, do your organization a favor, and do yourself a favor. If you are a school teacher, college instructor, or university professor who dislikes your job, also do society a favor by quitting, since you have no business teaching in the classroom.

If you are considering quitting your job, ask yourself, "What is the worst thing that can happen if I quit my job?" Then to the worst thing that can happen, ask yourself, "So what?" If the downside doesn't involve death or terminal illness, then say the heck with it all. It's not the end of the world. Put things in proper perspective; focus on the positive rather than the negative and life changes dramatically. First of all, you have your health and you are alive. Now think about all the options in your life. In North America, even without a job, you have more opportunity than people in the millions can ever dream about having on this earth. As for worrying about security, there is no such thing as true security from holding onto a job. Knowing you have the ability and creativity to always make a living is the best financial security you can have.

> *"It's good to have money, and the things money can buy, but it's good, too, to check up once in a while and be sure you haven't lost the things money can't buy."*
>
> *- George Horace Lorimer*

Think about the great things you can do between this job and the next one you undertake. You could sell everything you own and take the money and travel around the world. You could go to China and Rio and Mexico. You could go to Spain and paint. You could write the book that you always dreamed of writing. You could sleep in until ten o'clock. Of course, when it's time to go back to work, you may wind up with a much better job than you had before. Once you fire yourself, you may not want another job if you can somehow avoid one without severe financial hardships. Many people feel better about themselves when they quit the corporate life. Even many of those, who do not find something financially rewarding, say they would have a hard time returning to their old corporation.

There will always be some risk in leaving your job; everything worthwhile carries some risk. Besides, you may get fired sooner or later anyway. Remember, with downsizing so prevalent in the 1980's and the 1990's, the odds are increasing that your company will set you free, whether you like it or not (a good sign that this is about to happen is when you are given a secretary who doesn't speak English). By voluntarily leaving your job, you get to handle being without a job.

You are more proficient at handling the tough situation when it comes up again.

If you are going to get another job, don't be like the average job hunter who does not know what he or she wants to do. The average job hunter will take anything, or take a job because it offers opportunity for promotion. Instead, create a job that will be fun and fulfilling, and still give you ample time to pursue your personal leisure program.

The greatest risk may be in NOT leaving your job. If you cannot risk being fully alive, what can you risk? Going through the motions in your job means you spend eight to ten hours a day in a boring, joyless, and lackluster way. When your job is taking its toll on your spirit, body, and mind, it is time to get out, whether or not you have another job to which you can go. There are some things you should not sacrifice for any job. Your dignity and personal worth must come first. If your freedom is at stake, get out of the job immediately. No job is worth the personal sacrifices that will interfere with your enjoying life to the fullest.

Having Your Cake And Eating It Too

If you would like to keep working at your present job or career, but at the same time want a more leisurely lifestyle, you are an individual who wants to have your cake and eat it too. Here is some good news: Contrary to public belief, you can have your cake and eat it too. It's really quite simple; just get yourself two cakes. See! You are already ahead of all those workaholics and competitive fast trackers, because they wouldn't ever think of this.

Although optimal leisure is achieved by few people involved in the fast lanes of corporate America, you can be one of the people if you want to be. If you want to have your life in balance, first you must learn how to be a peak performer so you work fewer hours. As stated in Chapter 3, some of the greatest achievers in the history of humankind have been creative loafers. Peak performers get ahead by slowing down. They are not always busy because they know how to loaf. The key to being a peak perfomer is to work smarter, and not harder. How this can be accomplished in a job is beyond the scope of this book but there are some excellent books devoted to this topic.

Based on some studies about the available leisure time for the average worker, it appears a rigid career track offers little opportunity to properly enjoy and handle leisure. One such study - a 1988 Louis Harris poll - indicates the average American work week jumped from under 41 hours to almost 47 hours between 1973 and 1988. Leisure time shrunk 37 percent. This means less time for relationships, hobbies, vacations, and just plain loafing.

Other studies contradict the theory about less leisure. One study indicates, because of fewer children and less housework, the majority of North Americans have more free time - about 5 hours - now than in the recent past. The problem, according to these studies, is not one of not enough leisure. Instead, the problem is most people underestimate the amount of leisure time they have available, and don't use it constructively. Generally, North Americans have about 40 hours a week of free time. Behaviorial studies show free time is available, but most North Americans waste it. About 40 percent of it is used to watch television. Much of the other time is spent taking care of such things as cooking, cleaning, shopping for groceries, repairing the house, paying the bills, and doing work they have taken home from the office. It's simply a case of undertaking too much. The result is most working Americans feel less rested on Sunday than they did on Friday.

> *"Learn to pause ......*
> *or nothing worthwhile*
> *will catch up to you."*
>
> *- Doug King*

Regardless of what the studies say, I personally am not convinced that the average American or Canadian has no control over the decrease in his or her leisure time. If you haven't enough time to catch a breath of air, let alone smell the roses, it's probably because you are to blame. Practically everything in your life is a matter of choice. The lack of leisure time is mostly self-imposed; anyone who has too little time has simply undertaken too much in work or material possessions.

To have a better balance, you must get to work relaxing. Making time for leisure should be a priority. Many of the solutions are quite basic. One is simply to leave the office at 4:30 or 5:00 o'clock. You will have more energy to pursue other interests. In doing so, you will show you are an interesting, competent person and one of the real leaders of the 1990's. Also learn to undertake less in the way of tasks at home. Spend less time shopping, cooking, cleaning, and repairing the house. Many of these things take up too much of your time, because you allow them to.

Another way to make your career and life richer and more rewarding is to take an unconventional approach to your work, as does my friend Paul Brault. After having taught school for five years, Paul took a one-year sabbatical and went traveling. Now just four years later, Paul is finishing his second one-year sabbatical. Paul doesn't take sabbaticals because he dislikes teaching; it's just a case of Paul enjoying not working as much as working.

Conventional approaches to work arrangements prevalent in the 1970's and 1980's do not provide us with the best opportunities for optimal leisure and satisfying lifestyles. Progressive organizations realize that a well-balanced lifestyle means blending leisure and work. Leisure should be enjoyed when the employee wants it, and should not be reserved for weekends, vacations, or retirement. Here are some programs for enhancing employees' lifestyles which are gaining popularity in the 1990's:

- ⇨ Sabbaticals (paid or unpaid) for all employees
- ⇨ Phased retirement to gradually increase leisure
- ⇨ Telecommuting to reduce travel time
- ⇨ Flextime for flexible leisure and to reduce travel time
- ⇨ Job banks
- ⇨ Banked overtime which is used for paid time off
- ⇨ Job-sharing to reduce work hours
- ⇨ Part-time jobs to reduce work hours
- ⇨ Work-at-home schedules to eliminate travel time

These alternate work options are ways to improve the quality of your leisure time. Finding companies which support these programs may be difficult, but more and more companies are receptive to these new programs. If yours isn't thinking of adopting any of these options, it's time you found a new company for which to work.

There are other things you can do if you really want to have more leisure: Switching jobs or careers can open up possibilites for more leisure. Living closer to work to reduce commuting time is another option.

A balanced lifestyle means you have at least one quarter of your non-sleeping time unscheduled. Otherwise you aren't winning at life. Allow generous amounts of time for yourself to get to know and develop yourself. It is a mistake to put aside sports, travel, and active pursuits because of a spouse, children, job, and need to earn a living. You can always squeeze in leisure activities if they're worth doing. Just in terms of health alone, you cannot afford to discount creative loafing from your life. Having fun in your personal life will carry over into your work; your job will be more fun as well.

The most important point of this chapter is that you should be pursuing your leisure interests now. You may have to perform a remarkable balancing act to get a more balanced lifestyle. This may mean having to juggle your career, your debts, your possessions, and even your children. If you have a job that doesn't allow you to do this, then you should find yourself another job. Whatever you have to do, do it. Life is too short to devote to voluntary slavery.

If you are going to work, you should put emphasis on blending a lifetime of work and leisure into a well-balanced lifestyle. A balanced lifestyle with a satisfying career and many fulfilling non-work-related activities involves having your cake and eating it too. Having the cake and eating it too is not for everyone ...... having the cake and eating it too is only for those people in charge of their lives.

5. Unemployed: The True Test Of Who You Really Are

The Time Of Your Life To Have The Time Of Your Life

The intent of this chapter is to help you make an easy and comfortable transition to more leisure in your life. Many years of preparation may have gone into your entering the world of work, but little or no preparation is usually undertaken for leaving it. The time of your life to have the time of your life is when you are retired or temporarily unemployed. There is a whole new and exciting world out there without work. Being away from work allows you to enjoy life in a way not available to you when you are working. Not having to work creates the ideal time to enjoy leisure time, like never before.

The day you wind up with a great deal of spare time through retirement, or unemployment, is the day you get to test who you really are. Extra leisure time will be a gift from heaven, if you have taken the time to grow as a person, and if you haven't tied all your identity to your job. Learning to enjoy being unemployed involves the ability to experience everything through your own essence, instead of through the demands and directions of society, the business world, and the media.

"To be able to fill leisure intelligently is the best product of civilization."

- Bertrand Russell

It is just as important to handle spare time when you are temporarily unemployed, as when you are permanently retired. Career specialists say the general outlook is for people having to rebuild their careers several times in a lifetime. The average time spent on one job is now only 3.6 years. Employees are going to be more vulnerable to firings and layoffs than ever before. No job is safe anymore. The average 40-year-old white-collar worker can expect to change employers three times in his or her career, with at least one firing or layoff. If you are in between jobs at this time, make the most of it. Handling joblessness will make you more confident for handling it again when it happens in the future, including when you retire.

> *"This time like all times, is a very good one, if we but know what to do with it."*
>
> *- Ralph Waldo Emerson*

Your attitude and degree of motivation will determine how well you utilize extra spare time. The transition to more leisure is not always an easy one. While you are working hard, and trying to get rich and famous, you are not learning how to handle leisure. You are learning how to work hard, and how to try to become rich and famous. These skills are not easily forgotten. Even when you have the opportunity to relax and enjoy life, you may have a difficult time breaking away from your habits of working hard.

Writing A New Script For Your Life

Virtually everyone who loses a job due to retirement or unemployment is affected in some significant way. Those who say they aren't are either crazy, or are lying. Being fired, laid off, or retired is initially hard to handle for most people. As I found out, it isn't quite as easy as shooting fish in a barrel, or rolling off a log.

How much one has identified with one's job is a factor in how much difficulty one will experience away from a job. The greatest loss of identity accompanying the loss of a job is experienced by people who have totally immersed themselves in their work. For those who have tied their identities totally to their jobs, grieving the loss may take some time. Managers and executives normally experience a harder time during unemployment and retirement than blue-collar workers, because white-collar workers identify more with what they do.

Most of us have relied on outside forces such as the business media, universities, and corporations to provide a script for leading what society considers are successful lives. Conditioned by their own narrow mindedness, most of society's institutions haven't written into their script a way for people to handle a life of total leisure. We all will need to put effort into writing a new script for leading worthwhile and satisfying lives when we experience a dramatic increase in leisure time.

Although people nearing retirement have a fear of diminished purpose and activity, sooner or later most of them successfully make the transition to a life of leisure. Unfortunately, some people have been so rigidly socialized with unworkable Puritan values, that they find being without a job difficult, distasteful, and depressing. Due to their unhealthy attitudes and unwillingness to change, rigid individuals experience a serious loss of self-esteem, as manifested by the suicide rate for American men, which is four times higher in retirement than in any stage in life.

> *"A stiff attitude is one of the phenomena of rigor mortis."*
>
> *- Henry S. Haskins*

People who claim it is extremely difficult or impossible for them to have a worthwhile life without work are saying they have no essence. They are, for all intents and purposes, admitting that their personalities are extremely shallow, and their basis for existence is virtually all externally oriented.

I will assume you aren't so rigidly socialized that there isn't any hope for you; this is a safe assumption since rigid people don't normally read books like this one. In addition, I will assume you can write a new script for your life, which will help you make the transition to more leisure. If you have strongly identified with your job, don't expect instant breakthroughs. Allow the process to work since you will be remaking your self-image. You may initially feel like a loser, but this will change as your self-image improves. Your money-making goals have to be replaced with leisure-oriented goals. What you have to do is start changing slowly by getting some sense of accomplishment out of your leisure activities. Over a period of time, your self-image will change to that of a winner.

Rediscovering Your True Essence

With the end of a job or career comes the end of a perceived source of identity. If there is no new job or career to replace the old, leisure must provide a means to meet human needs where the job did so before. In making the transition to a life of total leisure, the first few days or weeks can be the most difficult. Some people can experience fright and panic; others feel the situation is unnatural.

An important factor for making a transition to more leisure is the discovery of your true essence. If you have been totally obsessed and absorbed by your work, you may have had little in the way of the leisurely life. In fact, you may barely have had a life .... period.

Your career may have provided you with most of your identity. You may have allowed yourself over the years, through the demands and nature of your job, to transform yourself. What is dear to your company may have become ingrained in you, instead of what is dear to you. Careers have a nasty habit of eroding our essence, or true self.

> *"There are two things to aim at in life;*
>
> *First to get what you want,*
>
> *And, after that, to enjoy it.*
>
> *Only the wisest of mankind achieve the second."*
>
> *- L.P. Smith*

Rediscovering your essence - what is important to yourself - can take a little time. This will take some digging around, mainly within yourself, to find out what makes you tick. You will have to show high intention by using your ability to grow, and learn in this new situation. Once you have discovered your true essence, you won't require the trappings of a job to define who you are.

Evidence indicates that with time most people adjust to being without a job, and find life to be as satisfying, or even more satisfying than with a job. Morris M. Schnore, a former professor of Psychology at the University of Western Ontario, conducted an extensive research study on the well-being of retired people. His findings, stated in his book, *Retirement: Bane or Blessing,* support the notion that people don't need a job for happiness and satisfaction in life.

After leaving work, the majority had discovered their true essence, and found retirement to be fulfilling. Only a small minority suffered from a prolonged identity crisis. Schnore found that for a small group (ten percent) retirement would cause a serious maladjustment. People with negative attitudes towards retirement are those to whom work holds a central position in their lives.

Schnore concluded that satisfaction in life was commonly found to be high, or higher, among older adults than younger adults. He discovered, contrary to the negative myths about retirement, retirees were happier and more satisfied with their lives than middle-aged workers. Almost one half (43 percent) stated their health had improved with retirement. Some retirees found retirement was better than they expected. According to Schnore, the factors which contribute to effective adjustment to retirement are:

⇨ Striving for goals which are attainable
⇨ Developing an appreciation for what one has
⇨ Confidence that one can cope with problems as they arise

Making a transition to increased leisure time means there are going to be many changes in your life. As you shift from work to more non-work in your life, you can't help but recreate your true essence. You will find there is no reason to feel incompetent, or worthless, just because you don't have a job. Once you find inherent value in leisure, you should have little trouble coming up with new ways to keep yourself challenged - with or without external influences.

A New Paradigm For Success

If you have always felt uneasy and guilty about enjoying activities unrelated to work, you will require nothing short of a paradigm shift to master the extra spare time accompanying joblessness. A paradigm is a belief or explanation of some situation that a group of people share. A shift from an old paradigm to a new paradigm is a distinctive, new way of thinking about old problems. Normally a new paradigm involves a principle that was present all the time, but overlooked.

> *"Success is having ten honeydew melons and eating only the top half of each one."*
>
> *- Barbra Streisand*

Your paradigm shift will have to involve a change of your beliefs about the nature of leisure. First and foremost, you are going to have to think of leisure as a worthwhile pursuit, as worthwhile as any job you ever had. A life of total leisure does not have to be frivolous and unfocused. Leisure does not equate to a lonely jurisdiction filled with boring daytime soap operas and reruns of *"All In The Family"*, although this is what it winds up as for people who hang on to old beliefs, or aren't motivated to take action. The realm of leisure can mean much success in your life.

The feeling of success is just as possible without a job as it is with a job. Success peddled by society means a good job, a big home, and a luxury car. This is not the only way to define success; success can be defined in many ways. With a paradigm shift, success takes on a different meaning. I like Ralph Waldo Emerson's definition of success:

What Is Success?

To laugh often and love much;
To win the respect of intelligent persons and
the affection of children;
To earn the approval of honest critics and
endure the betrayal of false friends;
To appreciate beauty;
To find the best in others;
To give of one's self without the slightest
thought of return;
To have accomplished a task, whether by a
healthy child, a rescued soul, a garden
patch or a redeemed social condition;
To have played and laughed with enthusiasm
and sung with exaltation;
To know that even one life has breathed
easier because you have lived;
This is to have succeeded.

- Ralph Waldo Emerson

Notice that all of what constitutes Emerson's definition of success is possible away from the workplace. Joblessness does not have to mean you are unproductive, or you are a loser. You are a loser only if you see yourself as one. As we saw in Chapter 2, perception is everything. You will have to change your perception of yourself if you see yourself as unproductive without a job. You can see yourself as a winner, because of your privileged state of having so much leisure to engage in the productive pursuit of self-actualization. Not many people in the history of this world have had this opportunity.

Remember that the great philosophers, Plato and Aristotle, adopted the right attitude in early Greece. The pursuit for leisure wasn't looked upon as laziness or uselessness. Total leisure was the highest purpose in life. Anyone who attained this state was definitely highly privileged to be able to practice self-actualization. Your paradigm shift should be manifested by your adopting a sense of privilege and opportunity to have a life of leisure available to you.

Reminiscing About Great Jobs That Weren't

The key to being happy to have left your last job is to overcome whatever nostalgia you may experience about that job. When we think about something from the past, often we think about the good things, and forget the bad. I know some people in the extreme, who even reminisce about things that never happened. In relationships, we remember the good things, much more than the rotten things that led to the break-up. Similarly, in jobs, we remember the things we liked, and forget all the things we disliked. Often we tend to miss the good old days that never were.

Let me share my personal experience about how I have been able to overcome nostalgia for former jobs. About four years ago, I still had some difficulty in making the transition from a 16-hour-a-week instructor's job to no job at all. Despite all my previous experience and enjoyment that I had received from many extended periods of total leisure, and the fact that this job only took 16 hours a week, the transition to more leisure was not as easy as I had anticipated. In the mornings I was raring to go, but there was just one slight problem: I had no place to go. I started missing the things that my last job offered, or so I thought.

> *"As lousy as things are now, tomorrow they will be somebody's good old days."*
>
> *- Gerald Barzan*

For the first two or three days I had misgivings about having resigned from this job. Nevertheless, around the fourth day, I was back in the groove. The feeling of prosperity returned. I started to feel sorry for people who had to go to jobs that they didn't like. I even felt sorry for those who liked their jobs. They couldn't possibly be enjoying themselves as much as I was enjoying myself.

"Nostalgia isn't what it used to be."

- Anon

One way I handled leaving this job was by thinking about the things I disliked about working in the last organization, as well as other organizations in which I worked. This quickly put my being without that job in proper perspective. Whatever nostalgia I had was quickly put to rest.

Exercise #5-1 - Telling The Truth About Your Last Job

Think about the most recent job you left. List the things you didn't like about your boss, your organization, or the daily events associated with going to work.

Based on the organization where I had the 16-hour-a-week job and other organizations at which I have worked, I have made my own list of the things I disliked about having to work at the typical workplace. Here are twenty five good reasons for feeling fortunate to be without a job:

Twenty Five Reasons To Dislike The Typical Workplace

- Being stuck in the office all day when the sun is shining
- Having to work with jerks and incompetents who should have been fired 10 years ago
- Power struggles within the office involving fierce competition, back stabbing, and paste-on smiles
- Getting less pay than someone who is much less productive but who has been around longer
- Commuting for an hour or two a day in the jungle of traffic
- Confined to a desk all day - the human body wasn't made to be this physically inactive
- Rigid dress codes that stipulate what you have to wear (i.e. that silly garment they call a tie)
- Constant interruptions and no time to think because of the daily pressure
- Paperwork - memos that mean nothing and reports no one ever really reads
- No cooperation by other departments
- Doubletalk by superiors
- Regular two-hour or longer meetings that go nowhere fast

- Excessive work load
- The organization expecting me to take part in social activities with fellow employees who are so socially deprived they have to socialize with people at work
- Too rigid vacation schedules making it impossible to take vacations at the best times of the year
- The organization asking employees not to take full vacation entitlement because of too much work
- Supervisors taking credit for our work and ideas
- No parking for employees except for over-paid executives
- Having to stay the full work day even if I am twice as productive as someone else and get my work done ahead of schedule
- Bureaucracy with red tape, foolish rules, illogical procedures, and unmotivated people specializing in dynamic inaction
- The organization advertising itself as being innovative but not supporting innovative people
- Discrimination because of race, sex, or being single
- Air conditioning or heating systems not functioning properly
- No recognition or acknowledgement for excellence in work
- Working with repulsive "yes" men and women who prostitute themselves for salary increases and promotions

Considering all the above situations are par for the course in most North American organizations, it's no wonder many people consider the workplace demeaning to the human spirit. If you miss your old workplace, think about all the above situations with which you had to deal. If your old workplace had most of these situations, and you still miss it, quite frankly you have a lot of problems. Put down this book now, and make your next destination a psychiatrist - before it's too late. Hopefully he or she will be able to help you.

Trenton, I am firing you because I can't stand obnoxious yes men like you.

Mr. Bole, I couldn't agree with you more. What a brilliant move!

Reading the above list from time to time should put things in proper perspective. This should bring a smile to your face in no time if you aren't working. If you are working, any smile you may have had will probably quickly disappear after reading this list.

Three Needs To Satisfy At Your Leisure

Most of us don't tell the truth about the workplaces we leave. After we leave a job, we don't necessarily miss the work; we miss the things the job brought with it. Although most people don't realize this, a job is more than a means for getting an income. A job satisfies many other needs besides money. Especially if we have a supervisory or management job, the job may provide us with many rewards: identity, self-worth, status, achievement, recognition, room for growth, and power. Upon leaving the job, these rewards are lost. Leisure will be satisfying only if it can provide most of the rewards which we find important. All our needs, which were previously satisfied at the workplace, will now have to be met in different ways.

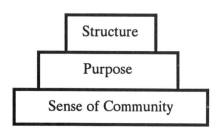

Three Important Needs

In this chapter, let's focus on three important human needs which most jobs inadvertently fill. The needs are structure, purpose, and a sense of community. Even if we work at a job which is not highly desirable, the modern-day workplace provides us with the means for satisfying all these three needs. Once we leave the workplace, all these needs have to be satisfied at our leisure.

1. Erecting New Structures

Structure is set by society for us from the time we are children until we retire. Tasks such as getting an education, working at a job, getting married, and raising a family all have ready-made structures associated with them. The problem arises when we find ourselves away from the workplace with substantial free time on our hands. Upon our retirement or job loss, the structure we had in our jobs disappears abruptly. Now we have to set our own structure. This means having to rearrange our lives which requires at least some effort.

Initially the loss of ready-made structures and many routines sounds great: not having to get up early in the morning, no need to rush breakfast, no meetings to attend on time, and no commuting in rush hour traffic. In other words, there is no longer a clock to rule us. The problem is most of us, no matter how creative, like at least some structure and routine in our lives. Being creatures of habit, we get addicted to structure. There is a great deal of comfort from the routines. And of course we all like comfort.

Having to lose structure and routine can create much havoc, especially for very rigid and highly structured people. Time must be filled to pass the days, but empty time can end up being the rule rather than the exception. Empty time results in boredom and no joy in living. These people may even withdraw from society and lead a life of desperation, because they refuse to adjust to an existence where they have the personal freedom to do what they want to do. In extreme cases, mental and physical capabilities rapidly deteriorate.

If you have learned how to be independent, creative, and motivated, the loss of structure will be a blessing rather than a curse. This is a time to enjoy your freedom and to create your own, new structures in your life.

> *"I'm trying to arrange my life so I don't even have to be present."*
>
> *- Anon*

Structure can be established in many ways. For example, I had to create my own structure and routines when I gave up the ready-made structures provided by the organizations for which I worked. Exercising twice a day to keep fit puts routine and structure in my days. I do stretch exercises for about 40 minutes the first thing in the morning. In the late afternoon I exercise for another one and a half hours by cycling, jogging, or playing tennis. Besides all the other great benefits I get from exercising, I get two and a half hours of routine in every day. I also put more structure in my days with activities such as regularly visiting my favorite local bistro to have coffee, chat with the regulars, and read three different newspapers. Setting regular time slots to write this book has provided me with even more structure.

Motivated people erect their own structures to replace those which existed in a former job. Self-made structures and routines can be established with the multitude of activities available in the world of leisure. Below are just a few ways to put routine and structure back in your life:

⇨ Take courses at your local college or university
⇨ Jingle your car keys at 4:00 o'clock each afternoon

⇨ Join the boards of charitable organizations which meet
regularly

⇨ Involve yourself in a sport such as tennis, golf, hockey, or
soccer which you can do on a regular basis

⇨ Work as a volunteer

When you destroy or lose structures, you must build new ones. No
one will do it for you; I certainly will not. How you deliberately
develop your routines and structures is up to you. If you have
developed as a person, your interests should be many and so varied
that the lack of routine and structure is not a problem. The task of
setting some routine and structure will be much easier if you have set
some goals and created some driving purpose in your life.

2. Being On Purpose

Many hard-working men and women know how to get things done
in the workplace, but find themselves lost once they gain more
freedom. With the loss of a job, self-worth extracted from being
productive and attaining goals is shattered. The reason is their purpose
is set out for them at work, and disappears when they lose their jobs.
They have never taken the time to explore themselves and find out
what they want to do, so they could set their own purpose.

Having a purpose when without a job can be a matter of life or
death. People without purpose don't seem to live as long as those with
purpose. Much of the literature on retirement quotes statistics
indicating that people without purpose in
retirement are not known for breaking records for
longevity. Seven in ten die within two years. The
average receive only 13 Social Security cheques
before they check out of this world for good. It
appears that these people, who have been addicted
to work, lose their purpose and self-worth once
they lose their jobs. If they had established some
other purpose in life, the purpose would have been a driving force
which resulted in their living much longer.

*"The secret of success is
constancy of purpose."*

- Disraeli

Your work may have been important to you. It may have been a
great creative outlet; however, you can make leisure as important.
Many activities can provide a creative outlet. Purpose doesn't only

78

have to come from a job where someone else sets the purpose for you. Without a job, a sense of productivity and achievement is still possible, but has to come from other sources.

When I was fired over 10 years ago, my purpose for the next two years was enjoying my life without a job or an educational institution to attend. I developed a passion for leisure and ended up with a sense of accomplishment, knowing many capable and intelligent people would have gone bonkers under the same circumstances. I could lay claim to going two years without a job and enjoying practically every minute. Because I did not have distractions from work and other events during those two years after I was fired, I learned more about the world and myself than I ever did at any other time in my life.

The purpose of skydiving is to see if you survive another day.

You must learn to focus on your purpose or lack of purpose. Discovering your purpose is the cornerstone for using your personal creativity. The biggest challenge will be looking within, discovering your purpose, and living out that purpose. A good way to find some purpose is to fill in the blanks to these self-discovery statements:

To change the world I would like to _____

Wouldn't it be great if I could _____

Someone with purpose who I admire is _____

At the age of 100 I would like to look back and say this is what I have accomplished: _____

I would get satisfaction in my life if I could _____

All successful people, whether at work or play, have found a purpose for their being. Here are some of the ways people have found purpose in leisure time:

* to make a difference in people's lives
* to make a contribution - i.e. community work
* to find creative expresssion
* to take part in discovery and challenge

* to help preserve the environment
* to show other people how to enjoy life
* to accomplish or achieve some challenging task
* to improve health and well being
* to create personal happiness and satisfaction

Meaning can be found in many activities available in the life of leisure. You can establish an educational mission or a helping-other-people mission or a self-actualization mission. With a purpose, you will have more energy than you can use. Stress will be reduced and your life will be in greater balance.

The key is to create a purpose for which you have a passion. If you can establish some ultimate goal or mission in your life, you will have a fiery driving force to keep your life exciting and interesting. This will ensure you are constantly growing and learning; your life of leisure will never be without purpose. Your purpose should relate to your essence and your dreams. Being on purpose means each task, act, and situation will be worthy of your total attention.

3. Generating A Sense Of Community

Beyond business, accomplishment, and power, the office has become a community centre for many people. The office is not only where workers make a living; unlike the past, the office is also where friends are made and after-work activities are arranged. An important component of happiness is a feeling that people are making a contribution to a community. Jobs provide the feeling that individuals are appreciated, valued, and cared for by co-workers. Often the need to be loved is also fulfilled at work.

"I will not join any club that will have me as a member."

- Groucho Marx

For many of us, the workplace is the only source of social involvement. A sense of belonging is provided in work groups, teams, committees, departments, and after-work activities. Work also provides the means for contacts which we require for socialization. The majority of us make most of our friends in the workplace. If we have been receiving socialization of 40 hours a week from our work for 35 or 40 years, it is not easy to lose all this contact. With the loss of the job, we also lose our best opportunity to make new friends and enjoy common interests.

Most of us also require some support systems for psychological and emotional health. For most working people, these are also mainly provided in a job. When they lose their jobs, most of these support systems will disappear.

If you have lost the socialization and support systems you had at work, you can't wait around to be discovered. The way to regain the opportunity for socialization is to contact new groups, associations, and organizations. Then you must get involved in them. Look to colleagues, friends, neighbors, family, new clubs, charitable organizations, and community leagues as a means of getting more community in your life.

What groups you join obviously depends on your needs and interests, but the important thing is to take at least two or more nights a week to go out of your home and into the world around you. Try to get involved with a group - large or small - which has a defined purpose. The organization you get involved with can be community oriented or it can be related to church, hobbies, or current affairs. In this way, you get to establish new social bonds. Furthermore, you get to have a purpose as well as the opportunity to attain recognition.

> *"Don't stay away from church because there are so many hypocrites. There's always room for one more."*
>
> *- Anon*

While you are out socializing, keep in mind that learning from others is an effective way of gaining wisdom in life. Find someone who is having a ball away from the workplace. Notice what it is they do. It simply makes good sense to seek the company of those who are good at handling leisure and living life to the fullest. You will see they create their own purpose, structure, and sense of community.

Making A Career Out Of Leisure

The day you wind up retired or temporarily unemployed, you have to look at leisure as a career. The rewards from this new career are satisfaction, self-actualization, and achievement of meaningful goals. You shouldn't feel you are worthless or incompetent because you don't have a job. Look at yourself as making an incredible contribution to society for just being able to handle being without a job.

A concept involving a career of leisure will go against many of your friends' or acquaintances' instilled values. Ignore any negative comments which they may make about your not working and not making a contribution to society. These comments come from mediocre or small minds. Learn to think of the sources of these comments as totally irrelevant or insignificant to your life.

> *"Great spirits have always encountered violent opposition from mediocre minds."*
>
> *- Albert Einstein*

If people are still not satisfied with your contribution to the world, let them know how much more motivated you have to be at what you do than at what they do. It takes very little ingenuity and motivation to go to a job where a structure and purpose are laid out for them by someone else. There is really a lot less challenge going to a structured job, and a set routine, than at handling a life of leisure where you have to create your own structure and purpose. You have to be a lot more motivated to plan your own days with constructive activities than to respond to something other people have created for you.

During my lengthy periods of not working, people have often asked me what I do for a living. I have replied, "Nothing. At this time I am too prosperous to work. I am presently a connoisseur of leisure."

When someone has persisted and asked me if I am financially independent, I have countered with my ace-in-the-hole reply: "I was talking about being mentally (and not financially) too prosperous to work. It is most unfortunate you haven't progressed to this state of mental prosperity, but I am sure with a lot of work you can get there." This normally shuts the person up and leaves the person in a state of confusion. This is the way I like to see anyone who is so narrow minded to think everyone's career should entail working for a living.

More leisure time should make you feel privileged rather than anxious. If you can discover your true essence, there can be great substance to your life away from a job. A healthy attitude ensures you will hold on to your personal worth and dignity. Without the confines of the workplace, you gain certain freedoms - freedom to think, freedom to reflect, and freedom to act. Your time can be filled with infinite possibilities. Remember, being without a job is the true test of who you really are ...... and truly an opportunity to become who you want to be.

6. Somebody Is Boring Me; I Think It Is Me

A Most Boring Disease To Have

Two gentlemen of leisure, a North American and a European, were discussing the joys of life when the European nonchalantly stated that he knew 100 different ways to make love. The North American, somewhat in awe of what he had just heard, replied that he knew only one. The European asked which one it was. The North American described the most natural and conventional way. The European then replied to the North American, "Most interesting, I never would have thought of that! Thanks a million. Now I know 101 ways."

Are you like the North American or the European? Do you see only one way of doing things or do you look for many? The habit of looking for one way, and the most conventional one at that, will set you up for the disease described in the following exercise.

> "He was known for ignorance; for he had only one idea, and that was wrong."
>
> - Benjamin Disraeli

Exercise #6-1 - Don't get this disease

This disease afflicts over 20 million North Americans. It can give you a headache or a backache. It can give you insomnia or make you impotent. It has been labeled as a cause of gambling, overeating, and hypochondria. What is this ailment?

If you at this moment have a headache, are reading this book because you can't sleep, and are deeply craving a giant five-decker sandwich after having just eaten one, you are probably bored. The ailment described above is none other than boredom.

Your transfer application states you are so bored at your job you have been falling asleep 3 or 4 times a day. Is that right?

Now recognized as one of North America's most serious health problems, boredom is at the root of many psychological disorders and physical problems. Some of the common physical symptoms of boredom are shortness of breath, headaches, excessive sleeping, skin rashes, dizziness, menstrual problems, and sexual dysfunction.

Boredom deprives people of the meaning of life and undermines their zest for living. Although it would seem to specifically affect those who are idle and jobless, those people in the workplace can be just as affected.

People who are chronically bored have certain characteristics. These people are:

* anxious for security and material things
* highly sensitive to criticism
* conformists
* worriers
* lacking self-confidence
* uncreative

Whether at work or at play, boredom is most likely to hit people who choose the safer, no-risk path. Because they take no risks, they seldom reap the payoffs of accomplishment, contentment, and satisfaction.

People who choose the path of variety and stimulation are rarely stricken with the ailment of boredom. To creative individuals who look for many things to do and many ways of doing them, life is tremendously exciting and fun. Just ask the European who now knows 101 ways to make love, if you ever run into him.

84

How To Be Really Boring To Other People

Boring people are victims of their own behavior. Unfortunately, everyone they associate with also falls victim to their "boring" behavior.

People who complain about themselves and utter trivialities are more boring than people who overuse slang, or try too hard to be nice, suggests an article in the November, 1988 issue of *Personality and Social Psychology*. Researchers, Mark Leary, assistant psychology professor at Wake Forest University, and Harry Reis, psychology professor at the University of Rochester in New York, went so far as to establish a boring index to determine which of the behaviors were deemed more boring than others.

> *"Some people are so boring that they make you waste an entire day in five minutes."*
>
> *- Jules Renard*

The following are behaviors cited in Leary's and Reis's study. Make sure that you adopt all of these if you want to be really boring to other people.

* Overusing small talk or slang
* Complaining about oneself
* Trying to be nice to be liked by others
* Showing no interest in others
* Trying to be funny to impress others
* Going off on tangents
* Talking about trivial or superficial things

All of the above behaviors tend to bore most people. Some of these behaviors are more boring than others. Reis and Leary found that the most boring behaviors were talking about trivial or superficial things and showing no interest in others. The least boring behaviors were trying to be nice and trying to be funny.

> *"Boredom flourishes too, when you feel safe. It's a symptom of security."*
>
> *- Eugene Ionesco*

We are all boring sometimes and most of us are interesting sometimes. Some people are more boring than others. The question is how boring are we to others; if we are boring to others, we are probably boring to ourselves.

The Real Cause Of Boredom

To a certain degree, we all get bored sometime in life. Ironic as it may be, many of the things we strive for can end up boring us: A new job in time becomes boring. An exciting relationship can become dull. Leisure time once deemed as precious may become dead time.

> *"Plato is a bore."*
>
> *- Nietzsche*

When we get bored, there are many things to blame: society, our friends, our relatives, low quality TV programs, uninteresting cities, a depressed economy, the neighbor's stupid dog, or a gloomy day. Putting the blame on external forces is the easiest way to react. This way we don't have to take responsibility.

Psychologists report that boredom is the result of certain factors. Some of the most common causes of boredom psychologists cite are:

* Unfulfilled expectations
* Unchallenging jobs
* Lack of physical activity
* Being too much of a spectator
* Seldom being a participant

A good question arises: Who is responsible for our lack of physical activity, our unfulfilled expectations, our being in unchallenging jobs, or our being a spectator instead of a participant? We only end up being bored if we allow these things to manifest themselves in our lives.

> *"In order to live free and happily, you must sacrifice boredom. It is always not an easy sacrifice."*
>
> *- Richard Bach, Illusions*

Of course, we are the ultimate authors of our boredom. We are the ones who must make our life more interesting, if that is what we want. Placing blame on people, things, or events seldom, if ever, solves our problems. No one else solves our problems but us. Eliminating boredom is dependent upon our willingness to take responsibility and do something about it. When we take the steps to avoid being bored, boredom is no longer a problem.

Dylan Thomas said, "Somebody is boring me, I think it is me." If you are ever experiencing boredom, remember who caused it; you and only you caused it. If you are bored, it is because you are boring.

The Easy Rule Of Life

People afflicted with boredom take the no-risk route because it is the most comfortable. All of us have the tendency to seek comfort at some time or other. In fact, most of us take the comfortable way all the time. The problem with choosing the comfortable way is in the long run it turns out to be very uncomfortable. This is best explained by what I call the "Easy Rule Of Life."

Figure #6-1 represents this rule. What it says is when we choose the easy and comfortable route, life turns out to be difficult. Ninety percent of us choose this route because short-term comfort is the most appealing. The other option is to take the difficult and uncomfortable route. When we choose the difficult and uncomfortable route, life is easy. Ten percent of us take this route because we know we must experience short-term discomfort for long-term gains.

Figure #6-1

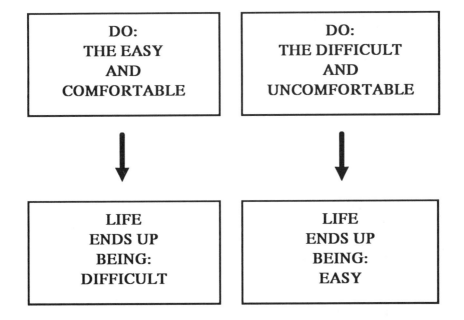

The biggest obstacle to success is the discomfort in doing the necessary things we must do to attain success. As human beings we gravitate toward less pain and more pleasure. Choosing the easy way ensures we wind up in a rut. And the only difference between a rut and a grave are the dimensions. In the rut you get to join the "living-dead", and in the grave you get to join the "dead-dead".

Let me warn you that the The Easy Rule of Life is something like the law of gravity. Mess around with the law of gravity by walking off the top of a building and see what happens to you. It knocks you on your butt. The same thing applies with the Easy Rule Of Life. Mess around with it by taking the easy way and you wind up on your butt as well. It seems to work everytime.

Everything in life has a price. Leisure with a difference requires effort. Most people take the course of inaction because at the time it seems the easiest. In the end they cheat themselves out of the big payoffs. Take my advice and don't be one of the majority who choose comfort at the expense of accomplishment and satisfaction.

Handling People Who Will Even Bore A Saint

We all have a boring acquaintance or two who seem to know everything there is to know about what is boring. These individuals can be just a little unpleasant and difficult to be around. If you are like me, after a few moments with them you begin to squirm in your seat and look for some means of rapid escape.

Clyde, you are boring me to death. I am putting you on hold for awhile.

To eliminate the boredom of being with these people, you must take responsibility. First you must get one thing straight: It is not the boring person who is responsible for your boredom; it is you.

One alternative for dealing with boring people is to find some way of changing your perception about those you perceive as boring. Your voice of judgment may be to blame. Often we expect too much from other people, and don't give credit where credit is due. To help yourself overcome the boredom of other people, practice being a saint. Look for something interesting and exciting about them. You may find that the boring person isn't so boring.

You may be thinking that this first alternative is okay for most people, but you know that one extremely boring person who will put anyone's saintliness to the ultimate test. In this case you have to simply take the necessary action to minimize your time around that person. In the extreme case, you may even have to eliminate him or her from your life completely. In the end it is up to you.

> *"There are more bores around than when I was a boy."*
>
> *- Fred Allen*

Boy Are You Lucky You Have Problems

Unwillingness to welcome and solve problems can add to boredom in our lives. Creative people look at most complex problems as opportunities for growth. We should all welcome problems in our lives as more opportunity to attain satisfaction from solving them.

How do you view day-to-day problems? Do you always look at a big or complicated problem as an unpleasant situation? Well, you shouldn't. The point is: the bigger the problem, the greater the challenge. The greater the challenge, the more satisfaction that is experienced from solving the problem.

Being creative means welcoming problems as opportunities for attaining greater satisfaction. The next time you encounter a big problem, be conscious of your reactions. If you are self-confident, you will experience a good feeling because you have another opportunity to test your creativity. If you feel anxious, remember that you, like everyone else, have the ability to be creative and solve problems. Any problem at hand is a great opportunity to generate innovative solutions.

Many things have been said about problems and how we should handle them. The reality of problems can appear to range from the good to the bad to the ugly. Here are some points to think about.

Whether the points are perceived as good, bad, or ugly will depend upon your interpretation.

You may dream of a problem-free life; nevertheless, it is probably not worth living. If you were hooked up to a machine which did eveything for you, all of your problems would be eliminated. It is unlikely you would find this as an attractive substitute to life with its inherent problems. Remember this the next time you dream of a problem-free life.

If you want to get rid of your problem, just get yourself a bigger problem. Suppose you had a problem of deciding what to do this afternoon. As you were contemplating your problem, a big, mean grizzly bear started chasing you. The small problem of not knowing what to do in the afternoon will have been eliminated by the bigger problem of the grizzly. The next time you have a problem, create a bigger one; the smaller problem will disappear.

"There is no such thing as a problem without a gift for you in its hands. You seek problems because you need their gifts."

- Richard Bach

When we solve a problem, often it creates more problems. This has many variations: Our problem may be our not being married. Once we solve this by getting married, we then get to enjoy the problems of marriage. Another problem may be our lack of enough clothes. Once this problem is solved, we don't have enough closet space and don't know what to wear. A problem of not having enough money, when solved with a lottery win, leads to many other problems such as friends not having anything to do with us.

Major problems involving painful incidents or major personal setbacks are often opportunites for creative growth and transformation. Many individuals report that going through a divorce or losing the whole wad in Las Vegas can give the mind a good rattling. The result is an experience of creative awakening.

Setbacks such as not being promoted at a job can result in a rebirth of creative thinking which had remained dormant for ages. Many people report that getting fired from a job was the best thing that ever happened to them. As indicated before, I am one of these people. Because of my major problem of being fired, I was given the opportunity to discover what I really wanted to do in life. Major problems are mind shakers that break old habits of thinking.

Putting Your Boredom At Risk

The last section stressed that problems are opportunities. The bigger the problem to solve, the greater will be the satisfaction from solving that problem. If this is the case, why do many people avoid problems more than they would avoid a pit-bull terrier with rabies? One of the biggest reasons is the fear of failure when attempting to solve problems.

Exercise #6-2 - Name This Man

Twice this person failed in business. He ran for State Legislature and didn't make it. Two times he lost in his bid for Congress. He did no better in the Senate races; twice he was defeated. Success eluded him when he worked hard to become Vice President of the United States. The woman he loved died when she was very young. Eventually this man suffered a nervous breakdown. Who was this man?

Many people avoid the risk of failure because they want to be liked by everyone. They feel that only by being successful can they be liked and respected. There is one thing wrong with choosing only success: Success only comes after a lot of failure. Take the example of the man in Exercise #6-2. This man was none other than Abraham Lincoln. All of his "failure" happened before he became one of the most famous Presidents of the United States.

> *"In order to get to the fruit of the tree, you have to go out on a limb."*
>
> *- Shirley MacLaine*

The best way for us to get rid of our boredom is to take some risks in our lives. By subjecting ourselves to the chance of failure, we put our boredom at risk. This applies to our careers and our personal lives.

Moe Roseb is an example of someone who put his boredom at risk. After having purchased my first book, Moe called me from San Diego to talk about the book and the power of creativity. In our conversation we discussed the whole idea of taking risks in life. At 46 years old with the children gone, Moe decided to take a risk and move from Eastern Canada to California.

He talked about how his friends of many years in Canada were rather boring. Some were having mid-life crises. Friends still saw Moe and his wife as being the same as they were fifteen years ago even though both of them had grown as individuals and continued to grow. Moe felt that his relationships with these friends had stagnated.

So did Moe continue to blame his friends for his situation? No. He put his boredom at risk and did something about it. He moved to California to new friends, new surroundings, and a new life. Moe looked at it in this way: "Many of my friends are having mid-life crises. I am going to have a mid-life adventure rather than a mid-life crisis."

Only Fools Are Afraid To Be Fools

On one hand, people in North America are obsessed with attaining success. On the other hand, most members of this society are afraid of failure and try to avoid it. The need for success and the desire to avoid failure are contradictory. Failure is just a necessary step to success. Most of the time you will have to experience many failures before you experience success. The road to success looks something like this:

Failure Failure Failure Failure Failure SUCCESS

The road to most success is paved with failure - failure and nothing else. Yet many people attempt to avoid failure at all costs. The fear of failure is associated with other fears such as the fear of being seen as a fool, the fear of being criticized, the fear of losing the respect of the group, and the fear of losing financial security. Avoiding failure means avoiding success.

> *"If you want to double your success rate, just double your failure rate."*
>
> *- Tom Watson*

Many of us avoid taking risks because of our fear of looking bad if we fail. We get so obsessed with being liked that we won't do things which we feel may make us look bad in the eyes of others. Avoidance of risk becomes the norm. This can be very detrimental to our creativity and to our aliveness. We must learn to be fools if we are to be creative and live life to the fullest.

Figure #6-2 - Fool's Chart

If you are afraid to fail due to your fear of what people will think about you, I have news for you: Most people are going to think bad thoughts about you anyway. In fact, when you are successful, they will even find nastier things to say. The more successful you are, the more criticism you will attract.

Most people's thinking about others involves criticism. It doesn't matter whether you are successful or not; you are going to be criticized either way. So what's the big deal about failing? You may as well go for it! Chances are you will eliminate boredom and make a big difference in your life.

The Fool's Chart above emphasizes that afraid of being a fool is on a much lower level than being a fool. Geniuses and successful individuals, whether at work or at play, have handled the fear of being a fool. They realize that in order to succeed in their endeavors, they must experience a great deal of failure, and regularly risk being a fool.

Being foolish is essential to life's mastery. Being "a fool" will put you on a much higher plane of personal growth than will being "afraid of being a fool." Success in life requires that you be a fool now and then.

Dare To Be Different

Being creative at leisure is being able to think and do something unusual. In this way you can generate something new and worthwhile in your life. This will take courage since you will be criticized and frowned upon for having the nerve to stand out in the crowd. If you have a healthy attitude, you will be able to ignore the criticism, or look at it as being totally irrelevant.

> *"To be a nobody, do nothing."*
>
> *- B. C. Forbes*

Making a difference in your life and in others' lives is a sure way to eliminate boredom. Keep in mind that you can't expect to be a conformist and still make a big difference. To make a big difference in this world, you have to start off by being different. Do something out of the ordinary and forget about what others think.

Albert Einstein, Thomas Edison, Mother Teresa, Mahatma Gandhi, and John F. Kennedy all made a big difference in this world. They all had something is common: The common denominator is they all were different from the majority of people. They were out of step with society; none of these great individuals were conformists.

> *"I would rather sit on a pumpkin, and have it all to myself, than be crowded on a velvet cushion."*
>
> *- Henry David Thoreau*

Don't be a carbon copy; instead be an original. Take the time to think about how you are limiting yourself in your life by trying to be like everyone else. If you have an unhealthy need to always fit in and be accepted by everyone, you are setting yourself up for a life of boredom. In addition, chances are others will find you rather boring. In other words, if you want your life to be boring, then conform and be dull; if you want your life to be interesting and exciting, then be different.

Boredom is something you experience in your life because you invite it in. The best way to overcome your boredom is to do something about it. Remember, if you are bored, it is because you are boring. The only person who can help you overcome this is yourself. You have the creative ability to make life exciting; use that ability. That's an order!

7. Lighting The Fire Rather Than Being Warmed By It

Dancing The Motivation Dance

Many years ago a young man mustered enough courage to ask a young lady to dance. After he had danced with her for a few minutes, the lady told him that he was a lousy dancer. She complained he danced like a truck driver.

For many people this experience would have been enough for them to have decided to quit dancing for good. Watching television or sitting around being bored would have seemed like much better alternatives. Nevertheless, this man developed a passion for dancing and continued to dance for many years after.

> *"I could dance with you till the cows come home. On second thought I'd rather dance with the cows till you come home."*
>
> *- Groucho Marx*

The young man did not quit dancing because he had the self-esteem and motivation to continue. He became known as one of the great dancers in modern times. At the time of his death in March of 1991, he had 500 dance schools named after him. He had at one time been on TV for 11 years straight, showing many different people, including truck drivers, how to dance.

By now you undoubtedly know I am talking about Arthur Murray. He became great at what he did because he was motivated to be good at what he did. Aware of his own ability to learn and grow, he discovered his true potential.

The Arthur Murray story underscores the importance of attitude and motivation; attitude and motivation go hand in hand. Only when you are motivated can you hope to accomplish what you want to accomplish. If you want to create a satisfying life of leisure, you must be able to dance the motivation dance.

Are You Motivated Enough To Read This?

You are reading this book because you motivated yourself to do so. The inducement could have been one of many: you were bored and had absolutely nothing else to do, you like reading books that stimulate your thinking, you are a masochist and like reading books you dislike, you read books like this one to put yourself to sleep, or you feel obligated to read this book because I bought you dinner last week. Whatever the inducement, there had to be one for you to pick up this book and read this far.

Motivated Tennis Player

Motivation is the act or process of generating an inducement or incentive for action. A lack of motivation will mean no action, and needless to say, nothing can be accomplished without at least some action.

It is generally agreed that unhealthy attitudes and lack of motivation are major stumbling blocks to achieving success and satisfaction in adult pursuits. Although skill and knowledge are important, they do not guarantee success. Skill and knowledge only contribute about 15 percent to what it takes to be successful. At least 85 percent of success is attributed to having a high level of motivation and a healthy attitude.

According to David C. McClelland, a researcher on achievement and motivation, only ten percent of the U.S. population is strongly motivated for action and achievement. The doers of this world have the "achievement motive." Although most individuals feel they have an achievement motive, there are few doers.

McClelland states the most convincing sign of a strong achievement motive is the tendency for a person, who is not being required to think about anything in particular, to think about ways in which to accomplish something difficult and significant. People with a strong achievement motive will think about accomplishment when free to relax with nothing else on their minds.

The difference between high achievers and low achievers is high achievers think actively and not passively. Studies on high achievers indicate they can take a lot of time to just think about things. Their accomplishment is not based only on being active physically, but also on their ability to meditate, ponder, and daydream.

Achievers think about being doers and attaining a sense of accomplishment. Eventually they do what they have been planning to do; this makes the difference in their lives. They know making a difference, whether in leisure pursuits or in business affairs, means having to light the fire rather than just waiting around to be warmed by someone else's fire.

Rocks Are Hard, Water Is Wet, and Low Intention Gets You No Satisfaction

Even though only a minority of us will motivate ourselves sufficiently to attain satisfaction in our lives, some psychologists say all of us are motivated at all times. There seems to be a contradiction here since I can think of many individuals who can't even spell motivation, let alone know what it means.

What these psychologists are saying is that everything we do is a result of some motive. Nevertheless, many people are motivated to do little or nothing at all. This type of motivation I label as negative motivation because it influences us in directions opposite to those that we must follow to win in life.

Victims of their own insecurities and past failures, people with negative motivation and low intention in life just go through the motions. They complain all the time, they start things and don't finish them, they make the same mistakes over and over again, and nothing around them seems to work. The saddest thing is they are not aware of how negative they really are.

> *"I learn from my mistakes. I can make the same mistake with greater ease the second time around."*
>
> *- Anon*

97

A desire for comfort and a desire to avoid failure usually result in low intention, or complete inaction. Although fear can be a positive motivator, it more often than not negatively motivates us to react in ways that contribute little or nothing to our satisfaction. Fear, for the most part, induces us to react negatively, rather than positively.

Other unhealthy modes of thinking such as the one-big-deal syndrome act as negative motivation. The one-big-deal syndrome is one of those adolescent-rescue fantasies we all had in our younger years. Unfortunately, I know many people who have carried these adolescent-rescue fantasies well into their 50's and 60's. Adolescent fantasies are favorites of adults with low intention and low self-esteem.

These are some variations of the one-big-deal syndrome: If I could only win a $5-million lottery, then I would be happy; if I could only get a new relationship with someone exciting, then I wouldn't be so bored; and if I could get an exciting, high-paying job, then I could start living. People afflicted with the one-big-deal syndrome are looking for an easy way to happiness, when none exists. Waiting for the one big deal is a way to avoid the effort required to make life work.

"Argue for your limitations and sure enough they are yours."

- Richard Bach

There are many other thinking patterns which can signal an inadequate intention in life as well as low self-esteem. If you have any of the following beliefs or thoughts, you are subjecting yourself to negative motivators that will contribute absolutely nothing to your success and satisfaction.

- I have problems in life that are unique. Nobody else could possibly have these whoppers.
- You can't tell me anything that I don't already know.
- I must be liked by as many people as possible or I will be miserable. When someone dislikes me, I feel bad about myself.
- I have a right to what I want in life and should not be subject to the discomfort of failure.
- The world ought to be fair, especially to me.
- All people are so different from the way they should be.
- Changing myself is impossible because I was born this way.
- My childhood will always affect me because my less-than-perfect parents are to blame for the way I am.
- Governments don't do enough for common people like myself.

- o I am disadvantaged because I do not have enough money, am not beautiful, and don't know the right people.
- o I am a good person who is nice to everybody. Why isn't everyone the same way to me?

If you regularly have any of the above thoughts, you are setting yourself up for much grief and pain. You are consciously or subconsciously generating excuses for not taking the steps you must take to make your life work.

Blaming the world for being a lousy place is a good way to guarantee that the world will continue to remain lousy for you. Even when you think you see the light at the end of the tunnel, it will be an oncoming train. You will end up giving credence to an old Norwegian adage: "Nothing is so bad it can't get worse."

Doing the following exercise will help put things in proper perspective.

Exercise #7-1 - The Creator Of Satisfaction

Spend a few moments answering the following questions:

1. Are you willing for your life to work?

2. Do you want satisfaction in your life?

3. Regarding your relationship with yourself, who is the source of the experience of your satisfaction?

4. Whom do you blame if you are not attaining enjoyment and satisfaction in your life?

5. To whom do you give credit when you are successful and experience satisfaction from your accomplishments?

6. In your life, if satisfaction is missing, who is not creating this satisfaction?

The intent of the above exercise is to remind you that it is you who is ultimately responsible for satisfaction in your life. If you tend to blame other people or circumstances for your present state of mind, you are putting yourself at the mercy of

> *"My life is filled with many obstacles. The greatest obstacle is me."*
>
> *- Jack Parr*

those other people and those circumstances. You must believe that you have control over the quality of your life; if you don't, people and circumstances will conspire against your success. You can't take the attitude that if life was a little easier, you would try to accomplish more. Life is the way it is and not the way it ought to be. Rocks are hard, water is wet, and low intention gets you no satisfaction. You must commit yourself to action if you want things to change.

> *"What is" is and "what ought to be" is a damn lie.*
>
> *- Lenny Bruce*

All of us at some time or other harbor the deep-seated hope that we will be spared the necessity of doing it ourselves. We hope that someone else will do it for us. Life is not that way; nothing happens by itself.

Everything of major importance, which you want to get done, must be handled by yourself. To be positively motivated towards achieving greater heights, you must find a way to eliminate all your unhealthy thought processes. Healthy thought processes are what constitute positive motivation. When you find positive reasons for taking action, you will be well on your way to accomplishment and satisfaction.

Motivating Yourself To Climb Maslow's Ladder

Several motivational theories have been developed over the years. Probably the most famous one is that of Abraham Maslow. His theory on the "Hierarchy of Human Needs" helps us explain what motivates us to do what we do in life.

The theory of the hierarchy of needs is based on three assumptions:

1. There is a definite rank order priority or hierarchy of needs that dictates our behavior.

2. The central assumption is that our higher needs may not be activated until lower needs have been reasonably satisfied.

3. We are motivated by unsatisfied needs.

There are five basic needs for which human beings strive. The needs in ascending order are:

Physiological needs - relate to the normal functioning of the body and include needs for water, food, rest, sex, and air.

Security needs - relate to our need to keep ourselves free from harm and include protection against danger, deprivation, threat, and insecurity.

Social needs - include our desire for love, companionship, and friendship. Overall these needs reflect our desire to be accepted by others.

Esteem needs - form our desire for respect and generally are divided into two categories: self-esteem and esteem from others.

Self-actualization needs - reflect our desire to be creative and maximize our potential.

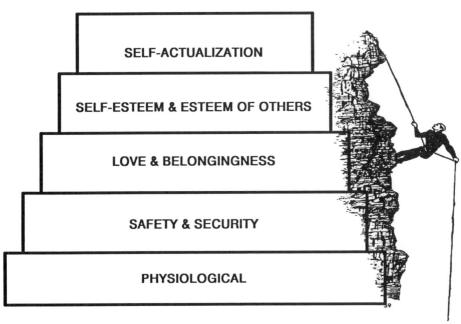

No matter who we are, our needs aren't static. Needs constantly change. Maslow contended that as our present needs are satisfied, other needs arise and then these new needs dominate us. To the delight of advertisers, no doubt, he stated that throughout our lives we are practically always desiring something.

We are best poised to enjoy leisure when we are self-actualized. Even when we reach the state of self-actualization, we can never consider ourselves fully self-actualized. A perfect state of not wanting anything would bore us to death. And of course it would be a nightmare for advertisers. We never reach a state of complete satisfaction except for a short time. As one desire is eliminated, another one is waiting to replace it.

"Only the shallow know themselves."

- Oscar Wilde

Our ability to satisfy our needs is dependent on first knowing what it is we need; we should know our needs well. This is easier said than done. According to Maslow, we may or may not be aware of our own basic needs. He surmised, "In the average person they are more often unconscious than conscious...., although they may with suitable techniques and with sophisticated people, become conscious."

All of us transmit signals to the world about our needs. Often this is done subconsciously. Our needs may remain a mystery to ourselves, but not to others who may be able to see what we need.

Exercise #7-2   -   Do You Need This Test?

Committing yourself to becoming fully aware of your behavior, attitude, beliefs, and viewpoints will go a long way towards understanding what needs you have, and what motivates you. Here is a test to determine where you are on Maslow's ladder. Although you will find Maslow mentioned in many academic books, you won't find this test mentioned in them. That's because the test was developed by a non-academic. The test is not highly scientific so don't take the results as being gospel.

Listed are some typical signals for each of Maslow's levels. These may help you develop a profile of the type of person you are. It will also show how far you have to go to reach the ideal state for enjoying leisure, that of self-actualization.

First do a self-analysis based on how you perceive yourself. Then try to see yourself as others see you. Since we have a tendency to perceive ourselves differently from how our friends perceive us, have a friend or two evaluate you as well.

1. Physiological Needs

- Not very energetic - is tired most of the time
- Little or no ambition
- Careless about dress and grooming and drives beat-up old car
- Prone to illness - hypochondriac
- Loner - avoids group activities
- Self-image is very low
- When working, has low work output

2. Security Needs

Tell me something! Is this self-actualization?

- Worrier - doubts own abilities
- Negative person who lacks confidence
- At work usually strong supporter of unions
- Focuses on poor income and standard of living
- Always concerned about retirement plans and insurance
- Avoids taking risks and has hard time making decisions
- Wears out-of-style clothing and drives older car

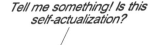

3. Belonging Needs

- Concerned about good grooming and attire
- Accepts invitations to virtually anything
- Is often a name dropper
- Wears up-to-date but basic clothing
- Belongs to too many clubs and organizations
- Is a conformist who always tries to fit in
- Takes part in team activities
- Wants to be liked by everyone

4. Ego or Esteem Needs

- Hooked on the external life
- Displays awards and trophies - highly competitive at sports
- Is often a name dropper of people and places
- Drives an overly expensive car with vanity license plates
- Carries a cellular telephone into restaurants to show off
- A competitor who tries to be one-up on everyone
- Wears brand-name clothing with lots of writing or advertising
- Is a doer who likes challenging activities

5. Achievement or Actualization Needs

- Feels secure and is very self-confident
- Creates own purpose in life
- Creative and independent - has rich internal life
- Definitely does not have vanity licence plates on car
- Accepts other individuals' points of view
- Good dresser but somewhat conservative
- Sociable but also likes privacy
- Not addicted to material goods for self-esteem
- Looks for quality friendships rather than quantity

Remember the above exercise is a non-scientific test I introduced in this book to get you thinking about yourself. I don't want you losing what self-esteem you have just because you or your friend evaluated you on the lowest or second lowest rung of Maslow's ladder.

> *"My inferiority complexes aren't as good as yours."*
>
> *- Anon*

Then again, there may be something significant to consider after taking the test. You should always be looking for areas where you can improve yourself. Only if you didn't have what it takes to make it to the bottom rung of the ladder should you show some concern. Even if you didn't make it to the bottom rung, there is hope for you. You would be surprised at how many of the rest of us, at some point in our lives, had self-esteem so low that we had to stand on our tip toes just to reach the lowest rung.

Many people with great natural ability have been immobilized because of their inability to get their esteem out of the deep ditch in which it rested. If you have low self-esteem, it is imperative that you do what is necessary to get out of the rut and raise your concept of yourself. With low self-esteem you will continue to experience frustration and failure. Low self-esteem is a paralyzing disease which invariably produces unhappiness.

The way to higher self-esteem is to change your attitude about the way things are and the way you are. If you can start achieving something in your life, your esteem is bound to go up. Achievements at leisure can be large or small; both will raise your esteem. With higher self-esteem you will be more motivated to go out and get what you want in life.

Do You Want What You Think You Want?

Only with effort and action can you start getting what you want in life. Keep in mind that filling your time with just any activity, when it may not have much meaning to you, is not the route to satisfying leisure. Your ability to enhance your life is dependent upon your ability to determine what your needs are and how you can best satisfy them. The following exercise requires you to answer a simple question.

Exercise #7-3 - Another Simple Question

What do you really want in life?

In his book, *Illusions,* Richard Bach wrote, "The simplest questions are most profound." The above question is a simple one with profound implications; it is not an easy question to answer.

Let's say, without realizing it deep down, you really want to stay at home for your summer vacation. For a change all you want is some rest, a lot of local sunshine, the time to read some good books, the coziness of your own home, and a daily visit with your spouse to your bistro for a great cup of capuccino.

There are a few problems: Your parents want you to go to Florida where they went. To convince you to go would validate that it was a good place for them to have gone in the first place, even though they didn't enjoy it all that much. Your friends Bob and Alice want you to go to the Rocky Mountains because that is where they are going. It would be nice for them to have someone with whom to have dinner, because they don't know what to say to each other when they are together at dinner. Of course, your travel agent wants you to choose an exotic place such as Aruba, Martinique, Bermuda, Puerto Vallarta, or Morocco. Your agent says she wants you to have the best possible vacation; the truth is she wants to make the biggest possible commission, so she can have the best possible vacation.

After 10 years of traveling to exotic, far-away places I realized I just wanted to vacation in my back yard.

You choose to go to Martinique for two weeks because the travel agent convinces you that you deserve the best possible vacation. Everybody who is a somebody is going to Martinique and you should show people you are a successful somebody.

Two days into the vacation, it occurs to you that you have seen all there is to see. You and your spouse lie on the beach all day being bored by watching all the other people being bored watching you. You only took one good book with you, which you have already read, and there are no good books to be purchased here. It is impossible to get a capuccino at the hotel where you are staying. The flight there and back is tiring, because of the time it takes to travel and the connections you have to make. When you finally get home, you realize that you didn't get what you wanted from the vacation. At the end of it all, you are more tired than when you left, and you feel unfulfilled because you didn't get the vacation you wanted.

One of life's most difficult processes is discovering what we really want as individuals. Notice that most of us don't know what we really want because we haven't taken the time to find out. The problem is we define our personal wants and successes according to the expectations of others. Societal standards have become more important than our own unique needs.

> *"Life is a progress from want to want, not from enjoyment to enjoyment."*
>
> *- Samuel Johnson*

We pay too much attention to what others want us to want. Society wants us to want. Advertisers want us to want. Our family wants us to want. Friends want us to want. Many others such as newspaper reporters, radio announcers, and self-serving travel agents want us to want. Everyone wants us to want so much that most of us haven't stopped to figure out what we really want for ourselves.

To further complicate matters, wants have a habit of shifting with the winds. Desires are shaped by hidden needs and reshaped by mysterious forces. Too often when we get what we want, we don't want it anymore.

If there is anything that will keep you from getting what you want, it is not knowing exactly what you want. Reaching the best destination is highly unlikely if you don't know what the destination is. You must do some soul searching and really understand yourself before you can determine what your wants and needs are. Only then can you proceed on your journey of fulfilling leisure.

Challenging Your Wants

Many of us have lost touch with what life is all about. We have sacrificed the child in us, which knew what turned us on for our own satisfaction and pleasure. Having given up our personal desires and wishes has dulled us so much that we are not stimulated by anything.

You may have sacrificed the things you have always wanted to do for so long, that you no longer remember what they are. If you don't know what your true needs are, you must spend more time and effort in self-discovery. Establishing your specific needs is something you can do on your own, or with help from others.

Ensure that you aren't chasing after what your mother or your best friend or Madison Avenue wants you to want. To discover what you really want, you must first write down what you think you want. Recording your wants is a way to make them more visible so you can challenge them.

Record your perceived wants by writing them down on paper or a blackboard, or by entering them on a computer. You have to dwell on what you think you want and find the origin of that want. Finding out whether you are the source of your wants, or whether it is something you were told you wanted, is important.

As you become aware of which wants are your own and which you were conditioned to accept, you will be better prepared to pursue your genuine interests. Perhaps you will find all of your wants were there because you were told you wanted them, or you thought you should want them, but really didn't. Then you have to look harder to discover your true wants. Don't shy away from this task, or you may waste the rest of your life doing what someone else wants you to do; this is not something which will contribute to a fulfilling and happy life.

> *"You are never given a wish without also being given the power to make it true. - You may have to work for it however."*
>
> *- From Illusions*

To repeat, write down all your wants, needs, and goals in terms of what you want to do and what you want to be. As you discover what you want, you can select those activities which truly turn you on.

Growing A Leisure Tree

"I'll try anything once, even Limberger cheese."

- Thomas Edison

The world of leisure is overflowing with opportunity. You can experience many different events, things, people, and places. The incredible variety in life offers endless possibilities for enjoyment and satisfaction.

A creative approach to selecting which leisure activities we want to pursue first involves the exploration of what is available and what we might want to pursue. Because our memories are not as good as we think they are, it is important to write all our ideas down, before we choose those activities in which we are going to get involved.

If you are like the majority, you normally use a list to record ideas. Writing your ideas on a list may limit the number of options you generate. Lists are not the best tools for generating and recording ideas. There is a more powerful tool, especially useful in the initial stages for generating a number of ideas for a project. The tool is an idea tree. Other names by which this tool is also known include mind map, spoke diagram, thought web, and clustering diagram. The idea tree is simple, but powerful. The surprising thing is most of us were never shown how to use an idea tree when attending our educational institutions. I first learned about it from a waiter in a restaurant.

An idea tree is started at the center of the page by recording the goal, theme, or objective for the tree. In Figure #7-1 on the next page, "Options For My Leisure" has been written in the center of the page. After the theme or purpose for the idea tree is recorded, branches or lines are drawn from the center towards the boundary of the page. On these branches are printed any principal ideas which relate to the objective of the tree. Principal ideas are recorded on separate branches near the center of the page.

Three important principal ideas should be used to generate ideas for leisure activities in which you may want to indulge:

1. Leisure activities which turn you on now

2. Leisure activities which have turned you on in the past

3. New leisure activities you have considered doing

Figure #7-1 - A Leisure Tree

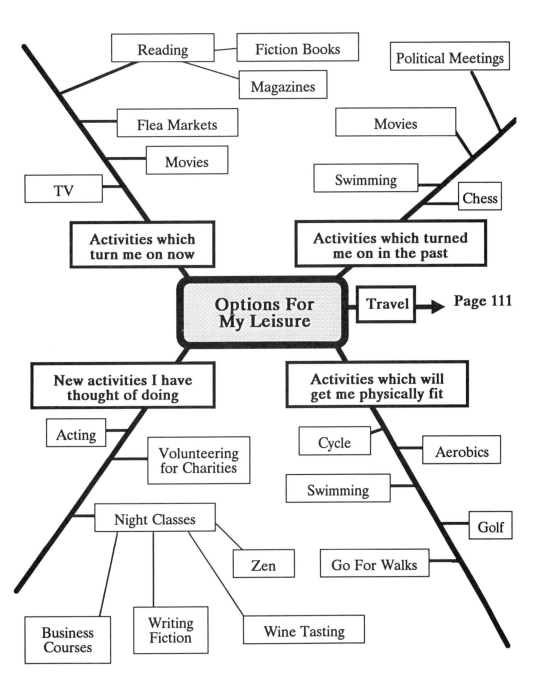

Secondary branches are then drawn exiting from the primary ones to indicate the various activities relating to the respective principal ideas. As indicated in Figure #7-1, you can add "Acting", "Volunteering for Charities", and "Night Classes" for the primary idea, "New activities I have thought of doing." More branches off the secondary ones can be drawn which will record a third level of ideas. "Zen", "Wine Tasting", "Writing Fiction", and "Business Courses" constitute the third level of ideas to enlarge on the night classes you can take. A fourth level of ideas such as "Marketing" and "Accounting" (not shown) can be added to enlarge on the business courses you may want to take.

Now is the time to start your own leisure tree using Figure #7-1 as a guide. Utilizing the first three principal ideas, make sure you generate at least fifty things you truly like to do now, have liked to do in the past, or have thought about doing but have never got around to doing. Record every idea, no matter how frivolous it seems. Don't judge your ideas here. You have to get at least fifty even if it takes you two days; forty-nine just won't do!

> *"Life is a banquet and most fools are starving to death."*
>
> *- Anon*

Other principal ideas can be added if you have special categories of leisure you want to actively pursue. For example, you may be very interested in getting fit and traveling in your leisure time. Then, as in Figure #7-1, you can record the principal ideas, "Activities which will get me physically fit" on one primary branch, and "Travel" on another primary branch. Note that if you run out of room, the idea tree can be expanded to another page, as this one has been for ideas on travel.

It is okay to have the same idea appear in more than one category. In fact, this indicates a leisure activity which may be a priority in your life. In Figure #7-1, "Swimming" appears in the categories "Activities which turned me on in the past", "Activities which will get me physically fit", and "Travel." If this was your leisure tree, swimming would have to be one of the first activities considered as a choice for those you pursue immediately.

Let's look at the benefits of using the leisure tree as an idea-generating tool: First it is compact; many ideas can be listed on one page. If needed, the idea tree can be expanded to additional pages. Second, ideas are put in categories and are easier to group. In addition, you can hitchhike on your existing ideas to generate many

Figure #7-2 - Enhanced Leisure Tree

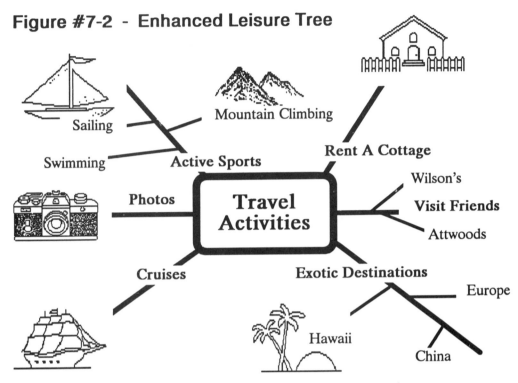

new ideas. Another advantage is the idea tree is a long-term tool. After setting it aside for a while, you can come back and generate a batch of fresh ideas. You can update it on a regular basis to ensure that you can choose from an endless number of leisure activities.

An idea tree can be enhanced by using color and images which add to our creativity and our ability to remember. Figure #7-2 shows a more advanced idea tree which uses images. As you can see, this looks a lot more interesting and useful than a conventional list.

After you have expanded your leisure tree to five or six pages, you are in a position at any given time to choose from a vast number of different things you can do in your leisure time. With any zest for life, you should have written enough to keep you busy for five lifetimes. If you didn't write down enough for at least two lifetimes, you have taken the easy way out. Go back and do it right! If you have trouble generating ideas for your leisure tree, refer to the list of activities on the next three pages. Your leisure tree should have enough on it so you are never at a loss for something to keep you occupied.

Exercise #7-4 - Ensure You Aren't Out Of Your Tree

Finding the right activities for your leisure-time enjoyment is a personal matter. You may overlook many activities in which you have been involved or which you have forgotten about over time. Here is a list of over 200 leisure activities for you to consider. Go through this list and rate them using the following rating system:

1. Turn me on now

2. Have turned me on in the past

3. New activities I have thought of doing

4. Have no interest in the activity

Activities in categories 1, 2, and 3 interest you and belong on your leisure tree. As you add these activites to your tree, they may trigger new ideas which you will also want to put on the tree. In no time your leisure tree should have enough to keep you from getting bored for a long time. With all you have to keep you occupied, you may not get around to finishing this book.

Activities For Your Leisure Tree

- Play an instrument
- Learn how to play an instrument
- Walk
- Run
- Volunteer
- Prepare a meal for yourself
- Learn how to cook
- Create a new recipe
- Visit present friends
- Visit old friends
- Try to meet new friends
- Go hiking
- Write letters to celebrities
- Take a survey
- Sleep
- Meditate
- Drive around in the city
- Drive in the country

- Count the items in this list to see if I have 200
- Read books
- Listen to the radio
- Watch television
- Listen to the stereo
- Travel
- Go to the movies
- Make a movie
- Learn computing
- Write a computer program
- Play tennis
- Paint your house
- Golf
- Fish
- Walk through a stream barefoot
- Go camping
- Climb a mountain
- Become involved in politics
- Ride a bicycle

- Ride a motorcycle
- Invite friends to your home
- Invent a new game
- Go to the library
- Search out your family tree
- Play with children
- Get on a talk show
- Offer to work for nothing
- Play billiards
- Dance alone for relaxation
- Dance with someone else
- Take dancing lessons
- Restore an old car
- Restore a piece of furniture
- Renovate your house
- Clean your house
- Telephone old friends
- Write a book
- Write in your diary
- Create a new cartoon
- Write your biography
- Make a dress, hat, etc.
- Try to create an interesting wardrobe for only $50
- Start a collection of ....
- Pan for gold
- Sunbathe
- Swim
- Have sex
- Go to church
- Dive in the water
- Go scuba diving
- Go snorkeling
- Get a pilot's licence
- Take up photography
- Develop a photo album
- Search the history of your birthplace
- Find out what was happening the day you were born
- Have a garage sale
- Rearrange your living-room furniture
- Take up acting
- Write a play
- Fly a kite
- Learn to run backwards

- Learn to impersonate someone famous
- Plant a garden
- Ride a horse
- Pick some flowers
- Write poetry
- Write a letter to a friend
- Attempt a record for running backwards
- Learn how to sing
- Write a song
- Memorize a poem
- Join an encounter group
- Learn famous quotations
- Memorize a song
- Gaze at the stars
- Truly experience a sunset
- Watch the moon
- Learn about new religions
- Build a house
- Design a unique house
- Go live in another country
- Go sailing
- Play hockey
- Build a boat
- Watch interesting court cases at the courthouse
- Learn more about the stock market
- Invent a better mousetrap
- Start a new club
- Window shop
- Learn how to repair your car
- Throw a dinner party for a variety of people
- See how many strangers will say hello to you
- Shop for clothes
- Watch people in public
- Roller skate
- Play cards
- Telephone a talk show to voice your opinion
- Have a candlelight dinner with someone
- Join a club to improve your public speaking
- Join a wine-tasting club to learn about wine
- Go back to university or college to get a degree

- Skydive
- Learn all about health and fitness
- Pick fruit in an orchard
- Visit local tourist sights
- Take up a new hobby
- Plant a garden
- Help fight pollution
- Go to a flea market
- Take a catnap
- Go to garage sales
- Climb a tree
- Go to horse races with $10
- Ride public transit for fun
- Start a newsletter
- Write a letter to a pen pal in another country
- Walk in the wilderness
- Do crossword puzzles
- Start and operate a bed and breakfast business
- Build a swimming pool
- Daydream
- Attend a sports event
- Travel to old haunts
- Go white water rafting
- Go on a hot-air balloon
- Be a big sister/brother
- Go to your favorite restaurant
- Try a new restaurant
- Have a massage
- Go to a tennis ranch to improve your tennis
- Teach your dog new tricks
- Learn a new trick to show your dog
- Attend live theatre
- See the symphony
- Go to a retreat to relax
- Truly communicate with someone special today
- Enter your favorite recipe in a contest
- Invent a new product
- Play with your pet
- Train your mind to be creative
- Run for political office
- Visit a zoo

- Make your own wine
- Kick the television habit
- Raise your vocabulary
- Learn how to read financial statements
- Learn how to judge personalities better
- Improve your personality
- End the evening by reflecting on your day
- Start a new charity
- Study clouds
- Make a list of all the successes in your life
- Play a prank on a friend
- Dream up new pranks
- Take twice as much time as usual to eat
- Go birdwatching
- Create a new game
- Try doing nothing
- Visit a museum
- Join a new club
- Go play bingo
- Fly a kite
- Skip rope
- Start an argument
- Watch someone work
- Lie on a beach
- Wash & polish your car
- Start a hobby farm
- Go bird-watching
- Help fight crime
- Experiment with solar energy
- Write a book on leisure
- Learn how to hypnotize yourself
- Have your palm read
- Do a jig-saw puzzle
- Visit a craft show
- Learn a magic act
- Cook a lousy meal for someone not to enjoy
- Learn to speak French, Spanish, etc.
- Care for someone ill
- Be a philosopher
- Harass politicians
- Expand this list to 500 activities to outdo me

Once you have created a leisure tree of activities, it is time to start doing some of these things. If you have enough for a lifetime or two, you must set priorities for those you want to pursue. It will be impossible to do them all at once. One of the ways to put a priority on what you want to do first is to think in terms of what you would do if you had only a limited amount of time to live.

Exercise #7-5 - Six Months To Enjoy Yourself

Assume you have been told you have six months to live. From your list of activities on your idea tree, select those things you would consider as essential for you to do in those six months.

The activities which you chose in the above exercise should have the most meaning to you. You should immediately start pursuing those you have listed; tomorrow or next week is not good enough. We must remember that life does not go on forever. None of us ever knows if we only have six months or less to live. By concentrating on the list of your favorite goals and activities, you will get to do what most turns you on and gives you the most satisfaction.

Goaling For It

If you were to walk in a clockwise direction on the walls of the object depicted in the figure to the right, you would think you were going up. It would appear to you that you were destined for greater heights. However, in no time you would realize that you are back at the same level at which you started. No matter how much energy you put into walking up the steps, higher levels would just be illusions. Your  unfocused activity would leave you without any accomplishment and satisfaction.

Such is the illusion of activity without goals and dreams. Many people misconstrue their unplanned activity for a direction in life. Even if they put substantial energy into these non-goals, they still end up getting nowhere. Activity is necessary for reaching greater heights, but greater heights only come with defined goals. If we are to arrive at new and worthwhile destinations, first we must define these destinations. The journey has direction once the destination is set.

Defined goals give us something to pursue which we otherwise wouldn't pursue; they give us purpose. When we have purpose and direction, we have reasons for being innovative and creative. Goal setting takes effort and discipline. Once goals have been established, more effort and discipline are required in working towards the goals. Then even more effort and discipline are required to monitor the goals and set new ones. Due to all the effort and discipline required, many people decide against setting goals and working towards them. Goals need an action plan to get us going. This tells us what we are going to do to get to where we are going. The action plan defines the activities in which we have to indulge while we pursue our goals.

If you have defined your leisure goals, sooner or later your wants and desires will change. Some goals will have been accomplished and some activities will no longer turn you on. This will necessitate a revision in your list of favorite goals and activities. It is a good idea to do a review every few weeks.

It is your challenge, and not anyone else's, to find, accept, and develop who you can be as an individual. You must face reality and accept that absolutely everything worth attaining in life - adventure, a relaxed mind, love, spiritual fulfillment, satisfaction, and happiness - has a price. Anything that enhances your existence will take action and effort. If you think otherwise, you certainly will be in for much frustration.

> *"One of the strongest characteristics of genius is the power of lighting its own fire."*
>
> *- John Foster*

Remember that it is more satisfying to climb mountains than to slide down them sitting on your butt. Sitting around waiting for someone else to light the fire doesn't work. Lighting your own fire, instead of waiting around to be warmed by someone else's, will make this lifetime (and other lifetimes beyond this one if you believe in reincarnation) worth living.

8. Dynamic Inaction Will Get You Nowhere

You May Be Living But Are You Alive?

A dull-looking man walked into the bar and said to the bartender, "Make me a zombie!" The bartender took one look at him and replied, "I can't ..... God beat me to it!"

Many people are like this bartender's customer. They spend all their leisure time in passive activities rather than having a good balance between passive and active activities. Due to their inactivity, they are not really alive. Neither are they dead; they are somewhere in between, zombies at best.

Dynamic inaction isn't the monopoly of a few bureaucrats with whom we have to deal. Many people practice dynamic inaction in their leisure time and it gets them nowhere. There is no limit to what these people will do so they can indulge in doing nothing or close to nothing. The problem is that after 40 or 50 years of boredom they are still in the same tunnel without any cheese, wondering when the plots in their life stories will thicken.

> *"Action may not always bring happiness; but there is no happiness without action."*
>
> *- B. Disraeli*

Having leisure doesn't mean people know how to use it properly, just like owning a car doesn't mean they know how to drive it properly. Over the years the pleasures of urban populations have become largely passive: watching videos at home, watching football and hockey games, and listening to the radio. There was a reason for people to pursue passive leisure in the past: Active energies during the industrial revolution were fully expended in manual work. However, this isn't a valid reason for most working people today; a vast majority of people don't work at physical tasks. Furthermore, the ones who still do manual work don't have to work as hard because of the machines they have at their disposal.

The main reason for most people being passive in their leisure is their laziness. Most people look for the easiest way to spend spare time. Even in the 1930's when people had to work harder physically, leisure was more active than it is today. People spent their time reading, going outside the home to movies, and dancing. North Americans have become a nation of spectators rather than a nation of doers. Individuals spend ten times more time watching television than pursuing active leisure. When people make it out of the home, they aren't necessarily more active. Studies indicate that, after the home and the workplace, shopping malls are the number one place where people spend their spare time. Researchers have determined that about 90 percent of North Americans today are reactive and passive. Instead of indulging in activities which are active in nature, they choose the most passive.

> *"Leisure may prove to be a curse rather than a blessing, unless education teaches a flippant world leisure is not a synonym for entertainment."*
>
> *- William J. Bogan*

What's wrong with passive activities? Quality leisure is dependent upon accomplishment and self-fulfillment, which come from activities that are challenging, or have some purpose. Passive activites seldom, if ever, give us the mental highs which do away with boredom. These activites are typified by no challenge, no purpose, low arousal, monotony, and lack of novelty. Although these predictable and safe activities provide security and safety, we get little or no satisfaction and self-fulfillment from doing them. If our passive activites aren't complemented by active ones, we won't experience quality leisure. Here are some examples of passive activites:

- ✗ Watching television
- ✗ Getting drunk or stoned
- ✗ Junking out on food
- ✗ Going for a drive
- ✗ Shopping
- ✗ Spending money

    ✗   Gambling

    ✗   Spectator sports

I want to stress that all passive activities should not be eliminated altogether. There is a time and place for many passive activites as well as the more active ones. For example, there can be a lot of good in just spontaneously goofing off, with no particular purpose in mind. Passive activities are okay when done in moderation, and when they complement a contingent of active activities.

> *"He did nothing in particular, and did it very well."*
>
> *- W.S. Gilbert*

Activity is essential to happiness and longevity. People have to realize that activities which mentally and physically involve the participants, such as going bowling or writing a novel, are much more exciting and satisfying than passive activities such as watching TV. Even leisure pursuits like daydreaming, meditation, reflection, and fantasizing are active in nature, much more so than watching television. Studies have shown that adults who remain active in leisure are more likely to exhibit higher states of physical and psychological well-being. Some activities more active in nature are:

    ✓   Writing

    ✓   Reading

    ✓   Exercising

    ✓   Walking in the park

    ✓   Painting a picture

    ✓   Playing music

    ✓   Dancing

    ✓   Taking a course

I always wanted to be an artist in my spare time. Now if I could only remember if I am supposed to use my right brain or left brain...........

Leisure should be something we all cherish and cultivate. It affords us the opportunity to have pleasure, enjoyment, relaxation, fulfillment, and achievement. Satisfaction in life is attained when we are able to challenge and extend our talents and abilities. This means the activities requiring at least moderate risk and energy will give us more satisfaction than those requiring little or no risk and energy.

A Case Of Mind Over Matter

Social conditioning can be a detriment to the leisure choices people make. A sure way to get old and inactive is to accept and adopt the thinking prevalent in society about what getting old means. Most people don't question what is said in the media, television, and books. Consequently, they believe getting older translates into having to give up most active activities. These people end up being affected by ageism, the existence of age-related myths. These myths support people in choosing a passive lifestyle after they turn 50 or 60, when a more active and satisfying one is still possible. Responses from participants in pre-retirement planning programs indicate that most people expect to increase their passive activites once they retire. Few intend to start new activities which are active in nature.

> *"What is mind? No matter.*
> *What is matter? Never mind."*
>
> *- T.H. Key*

Choosing an active lifestyle is mostly a case of mind over matter. Provided the person is not physically immobilized, age should not be used as an excuse to give up active activities. Here again, attitude jumps back into the picture. The person's attitude is important as to whether the person pursues leisure with substantial activity. Ken Dychtwald, in his book, *Age Wave*, looked at the challenges and opportunities facing an aging America. In the book, he relates the responses from the participants in his aging seminars to a question concerning what is the single most important ingredient in whether someone aged well.

"Invariably, they told me that in their view, the most essential determinant of successful aging is attitude. Each of us has the difficult task of steering our own ship through the challenging waters of life. Although it's good to have a sound boat, with a good motor and comfortable sleeping quarters, your attitude is in control of the wheel throughout the journey."

Dychtwald cites many people in their 60's, 70's, and 80's who are running marathons, playing tennis, swimming, and cycling for up to eight hours a day on a regular basis, sometimes every day. Unfortunately, these active individuals are still in the minority; most North Americans let themselves go with age. This is a conditioned response more than a necessary one. In the final analysis this can be attributed to laziness. The average US senior walks about 25 miles a year. Even the average Canadian senior, who walks about 75 miles a year, is lazy compared to the average Danish senior, who walks 265 miles a year. The most popular activity for people over 55 is watching television. A recent study indicates the average time an American adult over 55 spends watching television each day is 5.7 hours. In my opinion, this is about five hours per day too much, considering the overall quality in programming and the many exciting alternatives to watching TV.

Watching Television Can Get You Killed

North America's most time-consuming pastime is watching television. Like workaholism, excessive television watching is a harmful addiction. It has been billed *The Plug-In Drug* by writer Marie Winn. Although television can be educational and informative, there are many negative aspects associated with watching too much of it. This is what the authors (Rubenstein and Carin) who wrote the book, *In Search Of Intimacy*, said about television:

> "To us, extensive, solitary television viewing seems potentially more harmful than occasional, social marijuana smoking. Watching television is generally a substitute for social life, not a route into it."

In discussing the harmful effects from watching television, the authors went on to say that watching television in a group can be like riding a bus full with strangers. These authors didn't realize that television can be much more harmful than that; it can even get you killed by your immediate family. The UPI news service in December, 1990 reported that a Florida man's family confessed to trying unsuccessfully to kill him several times before succeeding. They eventually shot him dead because he was a miserable, grouchy man who spent all his spare time lying on the couch watching television. The man's daughter stated, "He'd come home from work and all he'd do is lay on the couch and watch TV. That's all he did. Like, he never did anything."

"I find television very educating. Every time somebody turns on the set I go into the other room and read a book."

- Groucho Marx

Exercise #8-1 - How To Make TV Fulfilling

Although watching television is a highly passive activity, there is one sure way to spend endless hours each month in front of a television set and still have fulfilling and rewarding leisure time in great measure. What is the one way? (See page 132 for the answer.)

Watching television is definitely a passive activity, not an active one. The mind is seldom challenged watching television. Another reason television is harmful is many programs and commercials depict life in a way which isn't real. This contributes to distorted pictures of the world, and fantasies about life that can't be realized.

Quality leisure time can be increased by cutting out television. The *Edmonton Journal* on March 5, 1988 reported Adele Amyotte and husband Paul bet $500.00 with their children, Donald, 8, and Renee, 10, that the children couldn't go for a whole year without television. In fact, Adele thought the kids couldn't last a week since they watched TV two to three hours each day. The kids surprised the parents; they made it the whole year.

Did the children suffer? On the contrary, they realized there was quality in life without television. Their marks in school shot up. Donald learned to pick out tunes by ear on the piano, invented songs, played hockey, and read. His sister played ringette and soccer and read. Adele Amyotte summed it up by saying it was rewarding for the whole family. The experience drew the family together. They spent more time with each other, played games, went to the park, rode their bikes, and shared a common goal.

Harold, you can't solve all your problems by watching reruns of All In The Family, and adopting the philosophy of Archie Bunker.

If you watch television excessively, cutting down on your viewing hours is an opportunity to enhance your leisure time. I can't tell you how much television is the right amount for you; it's your leisure time and your life. If you watch television to a large degree, and your life isn't what you think it should be, then doing something more challenging and fulfilling is probably the answer.

Don't Weight Too Long To Control Your Wait

No person is an island, but some people come pretty close with their constant nibbling on chips, tachos, peanuts, grass, trees, and anything else they get their hands on. Junking out on food is a passive activity in which many people get very active. Overeating goes hand in hand with television watching. Both activities, especially when combined and done to an excess, can lead people to an early death.

Life is too good in North America; far too many people are overweight. Even people whom we expect to be fit aren't. Up to 80 percent of some California Guard units called to fight in the Persian Gulf War were too flabby. Overall only half of the 2000 troops were able to meet fitness requirements for active duty.

> *"I went on a diet, swore off drinking and heavy eating, and in fourteen days I lost two weeks."*
>
> *- Joe E. Lewis*

Being overweight will interfere with your ability to enjoy many great pleasures in life. A good way to become overweight is to come up with excuses for putting on those extra pounds. Here is a good one if you don't already have enough excuses to justify your overeating: I recently heard a deejay on a local radio station report that a doctor claimed it was normal for people to gain three pounds a year after they were 30. This is another case involving people, both the doctor who made this statement and the deejay who repeated it, not having overworked braincells from thinking too much. This statement not only is ridiculous, but dangerous. If I allowed myself to put on three pounds a year, by the time I was 65 I would weigh 275 pounds and have a perfect look-alike body to match Dom DeLuise in the movie Fatso. The doctor's statement also suggests people in their 80's, who weigh a comfortable 170 pounds, must have weighed only 50 pounds when they were 40.

There are many excuses available for gaining weight. With excuses the battle against the bulge is easily lost. Although gaining a pound or two with age may be unavoidable, you can control your weight through exercise and diet. I have designated the weight I am comfortable with and have worked hard to maintain it at this level for many years. Your duty is to do the same if you want to feel good about yourself. The best way to accomplish this is by being as active as possible in the more active leisure activities.

Are You Exercising All Your Excuses For Not Exercising?

If you enjoy good health, you are in a position to undertake many more active activities than if you have poor health. Good health is a richness you should not take for granted. The way to maintain your good health (and your right weight) is through regular exercise. A study done by researchers from the Institute for Aerobics Research in Dallas, as reported in the *Journal of the American Medical Association,* showed strong evidence that physically fit people live longer. Even moderate excercise can improve your health substantially. Compared to the most fit men, the least fit men had more than triple the death risk. For women the least fit had quadruple the death risk as the most fit.

> *"Those who do not find time for exercise will have to find time for illness."*
>
> *- Old Proverb*

All of us have the opportunity to get fit through regular exercise. Yet only a small minority of us are fit. Joseph Arends, MD, in the practice of preventive medicine, states (as reported in the book, *Are You Happy,* by Dennis Wholey):

"Most people will never know complete fulfillment or be happy because they will never know what it is to be physically fit. It is an unfortunate thing over 97 percent of our females and over 50 percent of our males have never been fit once in their entire lives. Only 10 to 15 percent of our population is fit."

It is no wonder most people are not fit. According to the National Sporting Goods Association, there are 90 million Americans who exercise fewer than two days a month. They all have their excuses; the top five excuses in order are:

(1) Not enough time

(2) Not enough discipline

(3) Can't find an interesting activity

(4) Can't find a partner

(5) Can't afford the equipment

When it comes to excuses, pay heed to something Mark Twain said: "1000 excuses and no good reasons." If you are using the above excuses, remember these are not reasons. Excuses are for people with low intention in life. Using excuses is an attempt to falsely justify laziness. Let's look at the nature of these excuses.

The issue of "not enough time" is normally a case of poor time management. This can be handled by creating the time. Looking at things such as how many hours a day you are wasting watching television creates an opportunity to substitute exercise during those times. Of course, then you have to be disciplined to go out and exercise. The second excuse, "not enough discipline", definitely signifies laziness. You have to take action because no one can do it for you. It takes effort and practice to overcome the condition of laziness or not enough discipline.

Mom, how come Dad didn't want to come walking with us in this beautiful snowfall?

He mentioned something about how he would rather read about snowfalls than experience them.

"Can't find an interesting activity" is as shallow an excuse as there is. First, use your creativity. There are a thousand and one different ways to exercise. If you can't find one interesting physical activity, it is not that all activities are boring; it is you who are boring. The excuse, "can't find a partner", is also very shallow. This can be overcome easily by doing those exercises you can do alone. There are many such activities. If you can't do things alone because you fear loneliness, Chapter 10 provides some food for thought on this topic.

Using the excuse, "can't afford the equipment", represents limited thinking. Contrary to what advertisers want you to believe, exercising does not require expensive equipment. There are many things you can do for practically nothing. If you live in a relatively cold climate, as I do, be creative and think about various things you can do indoors during the cold days. The latest fashions in clothing aren't essential, unless you believe you may wind up as a contestant in a fashion

*"If I had known I was going to
live this long, I would have taken
better care of myself."*

contest while jogging or playing ball in the park. Advertisers want you to believe the latest fashions are important to you so you can make a statement about who you are. If you think you need the latest fashions to make a statement about who you are while exercising, new equipment or new fashions are definitely not what you need. What you need is a course in self-esteem.

Next time you are feeling down about something, try some strenuous exercise. This is what I do even though this is when I am least in the mood (I'm seldom in the mood for strenuous exercise). The key here is to forget about the excuses. Just go out and do it; this takes care of the excuses every time.

When we resist exercising because we don't feel like it, we need the exercise the most. Once we start exercising, it is never as bad as we thought it was going to be. In fact, after ten or twenty minutes it can become so enjoyable that we actually end up exercising longer than we had intended. There is a reason for this: While we exercise, our bodies release hormones called endorphins into the bloodstream. The result is a natural high which puts us in a state of euphoria. This natural high (medically called kinesthesia) helps eliminate that feeling of being down. Surprisingly, the physical activity eliminates the feeling of boredom, which made us feel like not exercising in the first place.

Exercise will keep you healthy and in a better mood to be more active in other activities. Individuals with good health are likely to pursue active leisure, while people with bad health are likely to pursue passive leisure. Exercising regularly and becoming fit will have a profound impact on your happiness and well being. Your physical skills and abilities will be maintained far longer if you get out and exercise your body on a regular basis. It is a case of use it or lose it. You can't stop the aging process, but you can certainly slow it down with exercise. The important point about exercising is getting out there and doing it.

"I like long walks, especially when they are taken by people who annoy me."

- Fred Allen

126

Smart Minds Ask Dumb Questions

We regularly condition our houses, we regularly condition our cars, we regularly condition our bicycles, some of us even regularly condition our bodies, but few of us regularly condition our minds. Regularly conditioning our minds can be as beneficial as regularly conditioning our bodies. Many people are in good physical condition, but their minds are not in great condition. The ability to think critically and creatively is a rarely developed ability. What passes for thinking in our society usually is no more than the regurgitation of old facts and figures that have been reported in the media or by someone else.

As children, we asked many dumb questions. We were curious and saw much wonder in this world. As adults, we can continue to challenge our minds with the new and mysterious. We should ask at least one dumb question a day. There can be much wonder and new things to ponder until the day we die. We don't know everything there is to know (although a lot of us think we do). In fact, dumb minds have an answer for everything, while smart minds regularly ask dumb questions. With so many interesting things about which we can think and ask questions, there is no reason for our minds to become rusty. If you can't generate your own mysteries to contemplate at this moment, here are four to get you started:

1. Why do we drive on a parkway and park on a driveway?

2. Why are your toes in front of your feet and not behind them?

3. Why does a cow stand still while the farmer burglarizes her?

4. Why is this question in itself a dumb question?

Another way to condition our minds is to take part in continuing education courses offered at our colleges and universities. Taking a course can be an extremely rewarding activity whether you are employed or unemployed. One of the most rewarding courses I have ever taken is a wine tasting course. Talk about enjoyable! It conditioned

> *"Universities are full of knowledge. The freshmen bring a little in and the seniors take none away and knowledge accumulates."*
>
> - Lawrence Lowell

my mind in a different way than other courses have. In what other course can you get to sip wine from a glass half an hour into every class, and learn something at the same time?

Here are some benefits from taking courses:

- ✓ Self-esteem is increased
- ✓ Great place to meet new friends
- ✓ Enhances personal growth and self awareness
- ✓ Improves mental dexterity
- ✓ Helps you prepare for going back to work
- ✓ Assists in handling the rapid change with which we have to deal

A creative mind is an active mind, and an active mind asks many questions. Only through active questioning can we keep our minds developing and discovering new ways of thinking. Questioning our values, questioning our beliefs, and questioning why we are doing things the way we are doing them should be normal. Socrates, a great thinker in his time, encouraged his students to question everything, including what he was teaching them. You should use your mind in active ways to ensure you are not letting it rust away. Here again, just like with your body, you must use it or lose it!

> *"Great minds have purposes, others have wishes."*
>
> *- Washington Irving*

Be A Traveler Instead Of A Tourist

Travel, when done right, will broaden and refresh your outlook on life. Experiencing new people, new customs, new surroundings, and new ways to live will enrich your life. The important consideration is to travel actively. If you can, avoid signing up for tour packages where a tour guide will take you from place to place. This is passive traveling; there is much more to travel.

Don't be a tourist. Instead try being a traveler like Paul Brault, my school-teacher friend, who takes sabbaticals every four or five years. Tourists are the passive ones who constitute the package-deal crowd. They opt for the one or two-week get-aways. On these package deals

they are constrained by fixed
schedules and the obligation to
conform to the group. Paul, as a
traveler, is more creative and
adventurous than tourists. He chooses
his own destination and isn't bound
by any schedule. Not having to
compromise for a group's common
purpose, he can take his time to
explore and enjoy the country which
he is visiting. Because he can be more
spontaneous, the vacation is more
unpredictable and interesting.

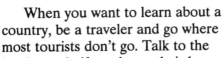

A drive in the country isn't too exciting.

This will be. The country is Mexico.

When you want to learn about a
country, be a traveler and go where
most tourists don't go. Talk to the
local people if you know their language. Learn how they view life.
Carry a camera and take many pictures. Record all the interesting
events in your diary.

Incidentally, when you get off the beaten paths and go to the
out-of-the-way places, you stand a good chance to find the excellent
restaurants not frequented by tourists. Find out where the locals dine
and you will be in for a culinary delight.

Another active way to travel is to get involved in a volunteer
vacation. This can be a fun-filled and rewarding experience. You don't
have to go overseas for this. There are many volunteer vacation
programs all over the United States. You get to offer your work to
organizations which can use your skills and abilities. The benefits to
you are the adventure along with the satisfaction you gain from
helping others less fortunate than you.

Try Reading, Writing, Or ....

Two more active leisure activities can
add immensely to the quality in our leisure
time; the activities are reading and writing.
Few people indulge in either one.

"The man who doesn't read good books has no advantage over the man who can't read them."

- Mark Twain

> *"Employ your time in improving yourself by other people's writings, so you shall come easily by what others have labored hard for."*
>
> *- Socrates*

Whether it's Duthie's in Vancouver, BC or City Lights in San Francisco, bookstores offer incredible treasures. There is also a literary gold mine in every public library. Reading books purchased in bookstores or borrowed from libraries is one of those active and satisfying indulgences everyone should pursue. Yet I read somewhere that statistics indicate the average university graduate in the United States reads about one book a year after graduation. Only three percent of the American population own library cards. In Canada, only twenty percent of the population spends leisure time reading.

Why a greater proportion of the population doesn't read books is a question I have pondered often. Most people may as well be illiterate for the amount they read. Apparently people find reading books too difficult. The Easy Rule Of Life from Chapter 6 applies here; doing the more difficult activities would give them more satisfaction.

Reading is the fastest way to gain knowledge and wisdom about the world in which we live. If you want to take the shortest route to success in any field of endeavor, then read the works of great philosophers. This is the easiest (and cheapest I might add) way to acquire the wisdom and knowledge that will make you a winner at work or play.

Writing takes a little more effort than reading. By taking time to write letters or books, you get to express your opinions and creativity.

I can't wait to get older, so I can be like the rest of the grownups, and read only one book a year.

Writing letters is something all of us could do more frequently. If you like receiving letters, then you should write. That way you will get more in return. Writing letters can be satisfying if you express your creativity. Add anything such as quotes or drawings that make your letters different. The person to whom you write will be pleasantly surprised with your letter, which isn't the run-of-the-mill variety.

Writing a book is more difficult than writing a letter. However, just

130

because something is difficult is no reason for not doing it. I encounter many people who dream of writing a book, but never get around to it because of their excuses. If you want to write a book, then do it. Here again, if I can do it, so can you. I should point out I failed my first-year university English course three times before I finally passed it; I am still able to write books. Start by putting in at least 15 minutes a day. This is how this book was started. Even if you do just the bare minimum of 15 minutes, you still will have progressed towards completion.

> *"Pardon the length of this letter. I didn't have the time to write a short one."*
>
> *- Mark Twain*

Once you have written a book, publish it on your own if you believe in it. Many books which went on to be bestsellers were self-published. But don't equate success with making it a bestseller. If your book is enjoyed by one person other than yourself, it is a success; anything over and above this is a bonus.

I feel only illiterate and lazy individuals are likely not to relish reading and writing. Of course, I may be wrong. You may not be lazy or illiterate and still not enjoy reading and writing. Then try something from the myriad of other active activities you can pursue.

Action Is Eloquence

Once you understand that your attitude and your energy determine the quality of your leisure, you will be on your way to creating the events and situations that help you live life to the fullest. William Shakespeare said, "Action is eloquence." As an action-oriented person, you will handle the inertia which stops the majority from pursuing active leisure. Overcoming inertia is the way to become creatively alive. Taking the steps to do something, which is highly active in nature, goes a long way towards eliminating depression, anxiety, and stress.

When it comes to life, two kinds of people exist: participants and spectators. There are those who spend most of their time making things happen and those who spend their time watching what happens. If you spend most of your time watching what is happening, it won't be long before your life is over and you will be wondering what happened.

Absent-mindedly pursuing leisure in ways such as watching endless television is a sure way to become bored and physically and mentally unfit. Always killing time will only serve to kill you faster. If your leisure repertoire doesn't include a good balance of passive and active activities, chances are you are not going to be very happy.

The best cure for boredom is finding out what you are passionate about and doing it. The activities from which you will get the most satisfaction are those which challenge you and provide you with a purpose. If an activity is really stimulating, we tend to lose track of time and place while we are doing it.

There must be several things you are passionate about. Maybe you are excited about mountain climbing or gardening or skydiving or riding horses or collecting old coins. The important thing is to have the enthusiasm which is so vital to getting you involved in something active. If you are passionate about what you do, you will show more vitality, more interest, and more radiance.

Exercise #8-2 - Measuring Your Passion

Go back to your leisure tree or list of leisure activities which you have considered pursuing. Rate these activities on a Passion Index of 1 (practically no desire) to 5 (burning inferno of desire).

> *"Be content to act, and leave the talking to others."*
> - Baltasar Gracian

After you have rated your passion index for these activities, make it a priority to pursue those that have a rating of 4 or 5. Anything less than a 4 is not something that will excite you enough to motivate you to pursue it with gusto.

With passion as the driving force, you won't have to force yourself to do these activities. If anything, you will have to force yourself not to do these activities. Passion, enthusiasm, and desire are what you need to get yourself into those activities which will give you the most satisfaction and fulfillment. When you are more motivated to do those challenging activities, you can't help but learn and grow as a person.

Answer to Exercise #8-1 - Make sure the television isn't plugged in while you pursue more rewarding activities in front of it.

9. Zen
There Was
The Now

Now And Only Now You Have The Now

Out of 500 people surveyed by *World Tennis Magazine* in a sex/tennis poll, 54 percent of the respondants said they think about sex while playing tennis. So what does this mean? It could mean a number of things: Possibly they find tennis boring. Maybe they are playing with, or against, some pretty sexy partners. How about a Freudian explanation? They are so obsessed about sex that they think about it all the time, whether they are playing tennis, eating a meal, sewing a dress, or riding a horse.

Now my real explanation would simply be that these tennis players just have a hard time living the moment. They can't be present, no matter what they are doing. The magazine didn't poll the respondents on this, but I would imagine some of these same people think about tennis while having sex. We will leave that poll for *World Sex Magazine* to conduct. It would also be interesting to conduct a poll to find out how many musicians think about sex while playing in a symphony orchestra.

> *"The day is of infinite length for him who knows how to appreciate and use it."*
>
> *- J.W. von Goethe*

Like the tennis players, most of us don't live the "now". We live either the "before", or the "then", in place of the "now". Many of life's most precious moments are missed, because we are so preoccupied with either the past or the future. The notion of living in the now isn't an overly profound idea; yet few of us do it.

Most of us walk around the majority of the time as if we were sleeping, paying little attention to what is going on around us. Some philosophers say most of us are unconscious most of the time.

If you want to be one of the conscious minority, remember now - and only now - you have the now. Being in the now is important because this moment is all you really have. There is nothing you can ever experience, except the present moment. Being in the now means accepting that you can never experience past or future moments. THIS IS IT! Believe it or not, now is all you will ever get in life.

Mastering The Moment

Lost, yesterday, somewhere between sunrise and sunset, two golden hours, each set with sixty diamond minutes. No reward is offered, for they are gone forever.

- Horace Mann

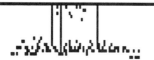

Being in the now is nothing more than enjoying the present for all it's worth. This is what Mij Relge, a very good friend of mine, has been able to do. At the age of 43, Mij quit his job as a university professor to do some soul searching, and grow as a person. Out of curiosity, I asked him what he was doing with all his free time, and what his plans were for the future. This was after he had been jobless for about two years. Mij responded with a Zen-type answer indicating he wasn't having any trouble at all with his work-free life. He replied that he was simply "mastering the moment."

Mastering the moment is important for enjoying leisure (and life in general). Quality leisure is dependent on your ability to be totally involved in the activity. Only then can you get full appreciation from what you are doing. This is true whether you are playing chess, talking to a friend, wading through a stream, or watching a sunset. Spending leisure in the now produces a feeling of vivid attentiveness, as well as a sense of real peace with the world.

Being in the now is emphasized in Zen, an Eastern discipline, which has personal enlightenment as its goal. The following Zen story illustrates the importance of mastering the moment:

A student of Zen asked his teacher, "Master, what is Zen?" The master replied, "Zen is sweeping the floors when you sweep the floors, eating when you eat, and sleeping when you sleep." The student responded by saying, "Master that is so simple." "Of course" said the Master. "But so few people ever do it."

Most people are seldom in the present moment. This is unfortunate since they miss out on many opportunities in life. Having presence of mind, or paying attention to the moment, is something upon which most of us can improve, and from which we all can benefit. The ability to be in the now and concentrate on the task at hand is a very important aspect of the creative process for both work and play.

> *"Time is nature's way of keeping everything from all happening at once."*
>
> *- Anon*

Essential to your mastering the moment is learning to do one thing at a time, instead of two or three. Doing something physically and thinking about something else at the same time are contradictory. You aren't free to take part in your chosen activity if you are thinking about something else. One of the problems we have with leisure is choosing something and sticking with it until it is time to quit. Any act or task should be worthy of our total attention, if it is worth doing at all.

Test your ability to experience and live the now by doing the following exercise:

Exercise #9-1 - Contemplating A Paper Clip

Choose a simple object like a piece of chalk or a paper clip. Concentrate on the object for five minutes. Your task is not to let any other thoughts interfere with your thoughts about the object. In thinking about the object, think about the form as well as the concept behind the form. Where did the object come from? Who invented it? Why is its shape the way it is?

Here is another good test for how well you can enjoy the moment: When taking a shower, try to eliminate all your thoughts about everything in your life. When you can get to a point where all you are experiencing is the pleasant and relaxing sound of the water running, you are truly experiencing a shower. When you try this, you will notice

Must be nice to
cruise around in a
Porsche.

Must be nice to
just goof off for
the afternoon.

how easy it is to think about other things, many of which rob you of energy and the moment.

If you didn't do what was suggested in Exercise #9-1, and instead kept on reading, you have shown how you are driven by your old self. So stop now. Go back and do the exercise! If you aren't able to do it, forget about being able to truly master the moment, and just be. You are driven by external forces which will continue to dominate the way you react.

If you did get around to doing Exercise 9-1, how did you do? If you are like most people, you had trouble with wandering thoughts. You became critical, judgmental, or helpless in doing and thinking about this ridiculous exercise. Having difficulty with this exercise indicates how your thinking often is very much out of control. However, you do not have to despair. Practice can help you overcome this. You can develop the ability to be in the here and now, if you want to.

The following three exercises will help you develop your ability to be in the here and now. Individuals who have used these exercises report improvement in their ability to enjoy the moment.

Exercise #9-2 - Concentrating On Better Concentration

Take a simple object and study it intently for 5 minutes every day. Concentrate on its form, as well as the form behind it. After two or three days, when you have totally explored the first object, use another simple object. Change objects as necessary. This exercise should be done for at least 30 days straight. The gestation period is this long, because this is how long it takes for our minds to change and develop better concentration. Every time you miss a day, you should go back to square one and try for 30 days straight. The benefits of this exercise cannot be explained in normal engineering or business school logic. Nevertheless, the benefits are real. Your subconscious faculties will open up to enable you to concentrate in ways you haven't before.

Exercise #9-3 - Clocking Your Concentration

Have the alarm of your clock or watch go off at various times of the day to remind you to be in the here and now, so you can enjoy the moment. Use this as a reminder to have the presence of mind to get totally immersed in what you are doing. This can be a reminder to truly enjoy your work by doing one thing at a time. It may be a reminder to appreciate the taste of food by eating slowly. You may be reminded to fully experience a beautiful sunset, or to be totally present with the people around you. No matter what it is, try and do what you are doing completely, instead of doing it in a mediocre way while your mind is thousands of miles away.

Exercise #9-4 - Control of Emotions

This exercise can be practised at any time and at any place. The purpose is to concentrate on your emotional feelings, anytime they occur. Whenever your emotions - positive or negative - are aroused, try to be aware of the reasons for them. Ask yourself what message the feelings are conveying. Why are you feeling this way? Do your feelings have to do with worry, fear, anxiety, or guilt?

Although this exercise seems to interfere with our spontaneity, it does just the opposite. This exercise helps us to get in tune with the messages from inside. In turn, we are better able to act upon what we feel without repressing any feelings. Spontaneity, which is discussed later, is actually increased when we improve our presence of mind.

The ability to experience the here and now is a characteristic of creatively alive individuals. Creatively alive people are those who can get totally immersed in a project. Their concentration level is so high that they lose all sense of time. Their project totally envelopes them - having distracting thoughts isn't a problem. Their secret? They enjoy the moment for what it is, and don't worry about what is coming up next.

"Nothing is so dear and precious as time."

- French Proverb

137

Have you ever been possessed by an energy that carried you away from your normal concerns into a state of optimal satisfaction? If you have, you were mastering the moment and may have experienced numerous feelings which you normally don't experience. Two professors of psychology at Southern Illinois University, Howard E.A. Tinsley and Diane J. Tinsley, found individuals experiencing leisure to the fullest felt the following:

- ☆ A feeling of freedom
- ☆ Total absorption in the activity at hand
- ☆ Lack of focus on self
- ☆ Enhanced perception of objects and events
- ☆ Little awareness of the passage of time
- ☆ Increased sensitivity to body sensations
- ☆ Increased sensitivity to emotions

The secret to being happy at your leisure is to frequently participate in activities in which you master the moment. You will be carried away by experiences that are extraordinarily joyous, fulfilling, and meaningful. Mastering the moment is spending an afternoon browsing without a definite purpose in a library, or writing a letter by hand that flows on with endless ideas. It is the experience of doing something with so much fascination and enjoyment that you lose all sense of time and place. When you are mastering the moment, nothing is important, except what you are doing at that time.

Ultimately Nothing Matters And So What If It Did

Worrying about the trivial or important is one of the activities which robs people of the now. About 15 percent of the US public spends at least 50 percent of each day worrying says a study from Pennsylvania State University. Worry is so rampant in North America that certain researchers claim approximately one out of three people in North American society has serious mental problems as a result of worrying. On that note, think of two of your friends. If you consider both of them mentally

> *"I am an old man and have known a great many troubles, but most of them never happened."*
>
> *- Mark Twain*

138

healthy, then you must be the one out of the three with the mental problems (I'm just kidding).

To put worrying in proper perspective, the following story is another one told in Zen teachings:

> Two monks, Eanzan and Tekido, were walking along a muddy road when they came upon a beautiful woman unable to cross the road without getting her silk shoes muddy. Without saying a word, Eanzan picked up and carried the woman across the road, leaving her on the other side. Then the two monks continued walking without talking until the end of the day. When they reached their destination, Tekido said, "You know monks are supposed to avoid women. Why did you pick up that woman this morning?" Eanzan replied, "I left her on the side of the road. Why are you at this time still carrying her?"

The above story emphasizes the Zen philosophy about the importance of going through life not carrying around problems from the past. Yet many people focus on former problems. Worrying comprises most of people's thinking with some people so used to worrying that they worry if they don't have anything to worry about.

Exercise #9-5 - Two Days About Which Not To Worry

There are two days of the week about which you should not worry. What are these two days?

Fear, anxiety, and guilt are emotions related to worrying. At any given time, at work or elsewhere, people's minds are far, far away - mostly thinking about worries and regrets. Most people are worrying about what happened yesterday or what will happen tomorrow. This leads to the answer for Exercise #9-5: The two days of the week about which you should not worry are

> "It isn't the experience of today that drives men mad. It is the remorse for something that happened yesterday, and the dread of what tomorrow may disclose."
>
> - Robert Jones Burdette

tomorrow and yesterday.

Are you spending too much time worrying and missing out on today? Can you concentrate and be in the here and now? Spending too much time worrying about losing, failing, or making mistakes will make you tense and anxious. Too much worrying predisposes you to stress, headaches, panic attacks, ulcers, and other related ailments. Most worry is self-inflicted and somewhat useless. Just consider the following chart:

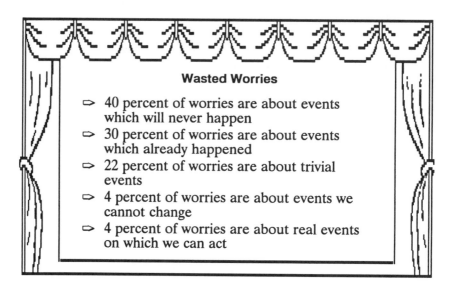

Wasted Worries

▷ 40 percent of worries are about events which will never happen
▷ 30 percent of worries are about events which already happened
▷ 22 percent of worries are about trivial events
▷ 4 percent of worries are about events we cannot change
▷ 4 percent of worries are about real events on which we can act

The above chart indicates that 96 percent of the energy we spend on worrying is used on things we cannot control. This signifies 96 percent of our worrying is wasted. In fact, it is even worse than that. Worrying about things we can control is wasted as well, since we can control these things. In other words, worrying about things we can't control is wasted because we can't control them, and worrying about things we can control is wasted because we can control these things. The result is 100 percent of our worrying is wasted. (Now you can worry about all the time you have been wasting while worrying.)

Spending time worrying about past happenings or future concerns is a waste of energy. Creative people realize Murphy's law has some bearing on the way things will be; that is, "If anything can go wrong, it will." Hurdles are a certainty in life. There is no way for the highly creative to eliminate all the hurdles. They realize many new hurdles will appear regularly, but they also realize there is a way to overcome virtually all hurdles.

When a hurdle appears, creative people will figure out a way to eliminate the hurdle. If they can't get over it, they will go under it. If they can't get under it, they will go around it. If they can't go around it, they will go through it. With all these options, there is no need to worry about hurdles. What is important is whether or not there is a hurdle now. If there isn't one, fine. If there is one, fine again, because there is a challenge to face and a new problem to solve.

Most, if not all, worrying about problems robs you of energy which can be channelled to solve these problems. Here is a good attitude for you to adopt: Ultimately nothing matters and so what if it did. If you can live this motto, most worries will be eliminated.

Giving Up Control To Be In Control

Many people say they want to be in total control at all times. They worry and are insecure when they feel out of control. The need for control can be self-defeating. The creatively alive people of this world say one important factor for being fully alive is having the ability to yield or give up the need to control. Of course, this goes against what we have allowed ourselves to believe.

> "The world is ruled by letting things take their course. It cannot be ruled by interfering."
>
> - Lao Tsu

If you have ever ridden a horse, you will have realized it is much easier to ride the horse in the direction it is going. Getting through life in this world is also easier if you ride with the world in the direction it's going. This means giving up the need to control the way everything is going to turn out. To illustrate the importance of giving up control in life, I find it useful to use this analogy:

Assume you are on a raft floating down a fast moving and highly treacherous river. The raft happens to capsize and you fall into the rapidly flowing water. There are two things you can do. One is to try and take control and fight the river. If you do this you are liable to end up injured, as a result of being thrown against the rocks. The second thing you can do is give up total control. The moment you give up control you will be in control. You are now going with the flow. The water doesn't go into the rocks. The water goes around the rocks.

Life is a fast moving river. To get through life with a minimum of scrapes and bruises, we must learn how to go with the flow. Going with the flow means giving up control. It means surrendering to the notion that we don't know how anything is going to turn out. The best way to be in control of our destinies is to give up control and not worry about how things are going to turn out. Too many factors beyond our control will destroy the best of plans.

> *"When you have got an elephant by the hind leg, and he is trying to run away, it's best to let him run."*
>
> *- Abraham Lincoln*

Creatively alive people yield and go with the flow. In going with the flow, creatively alive people are acknowledging the importance of mastering the moment.

Don't Plan To Be Spontaneous

Unlike the majority of adults, creatively alive adults live the moment. Similarly, unlike the majority of adults, creatively alive adults can be spontaneous. I think Mark Twain was probably speaking of his lack of spontaneity as an adult when he said, "It usually takes me more than three weeks to prepare a good impromptu speech."

Abraham Maslow, the famous humanist physchologist, believed spontaneity is a trait which is too often lost as people grow older. Maslow said, "Almost any child can compose a song or poem or a dance or a painting or a play or a game on the spur of the moment, without planning or previous intent." The majority of adults lose this ability, according to Maslow. Nevertheless, Maslow found a small fraction of adults did not lose this trait, and if they did, they regained it later in life. These were the people who were self-actualized. Recall from Chapter 7 that self-actualization is the state of outstanding mental health. Maslow called this a state of being fully human. He found self-actualized people to be spontaneous and highly creative while moving toward maturity.

Spontaneity is, for all intents and purposes, synonymous with creative living. Creatively alive people aren't inhibited; they can express their true feelings. They are able, like children, to play and act foolish. They also are able, on the spur of the moment, to decide to do something not in their plans for that day. Creative people also have no problem with impromptu speeches. They are more like children when they speak, rather than like adults.

I had planned to be spontaneous today at 3:00 o'clock, but I'm swamped. It looks like I will have to reschedule it for tomorrow.

How spontaneous are you? Do you always stick to your plans for the day? Do you always follow a set routine? How often do you ignore your plans and do something different? I have found that when I do something spontaneous, unexpected and interesting things happen to me. Many times I wind up with rewarding experiences which I would have never achieved by sticking to my plans.

Watch children to refresh your notion of spontaneity. If you can be a child again, you can be spontaneous. Being spontaneous means challenging your plans; it means being able to try something new on the spur of the moment because it may be something you will enjoy. Although most accountants and engineers would probably try to plan to be more spontaneous, no one can plan spontaneity. "Planned spontaneity" is an oxymoron; spontaneous means unplanned.

Being spontaneous also means allowing more chance in your life. The more chance you let in your world, the more interesting your world of leisure will become. Let more people in your life. Communicate with them and express yourself to them, especially if they have a different viewpoint from your own. You might learn something new.

Remember to be spontaneous on a regular basis. Every day practice doing something which you haven't planned. On the spur of the moment, choose and do something new and exciting. It can be quite a small thing like taking a different route somewhere, eating in a different restaurant, or going to some new kind of entertainment. You can make your life of leisure much more interesting by introducing something novel in all your activities.

Living Happily Ever After On A Day-To-Day Basis

Some time ago I encountered a semi-derelict walking out of a third-rate hotel in the morning. There wasn't anyone with him at the time, and he was unaware of my presence. I overheard him say with great joy and enthusiasm, "Good morning world, how are you?" Then he looked at the surroundings and the bright sun, and said with a glow in his face, "Amazing, just amazing!"

I was in awe of this man. He was able to show great joy, although he didn't seem to have the many other things people strive for in our society. When I saw how happy he was to be alive, I was surprised he wasn't levitating. Then I thought about the thousands of miserable faces I would have seen if I had been downtown that morning. It would have been difficult for me to find one employed person showing so much joy, just for just being alive that day. The faces I would have encountered would have displayed the seriousness normally seen on the faces of musicians playing in a symphony orchestra. And I am sure if I was to hear their conversations, most wouldn't have been about happy events.

> *"We have no more right to consume happiness without producing it, than to consume wealth without producing it."*
>
> *- George Bernard Shaw*

Abraham Lincoln said most folks are about as happy as they make up their minds to be. I am sure the semi-derilect whom I encountered that morning would have said the same thing. So there you have it folks; you're about as happy as you want to be. For centuries great thinkers and religious leaders from different faiths have been saying basically the same thing about happiness. They could shout it from the rooftops and cast it in every stone; most people still won't get it. Happiness is on the inside, not on the outside. True happiness is finding contentment within oneself. All the possessions in the world are not going to bring anyone the happiness that some people with virtually no possessions experience from within.

My goals in life are to be happy, live every moment for all it's worth, and learn to do one thing at a time.

One common goal in life is to be happy. Just like the fictitious characters we read about in fairy tales when we were children, most people would like to live happily ever after. They want to have nothing but good times.

Life can only be lived happily ever after on a day-to-day basis. Happiness is something which happens in the now. If your primary goal in life is to be happy, happiness will elude you. Happiness is a product of achieving goals, but not a goal in itself.

Having as many good times as possible is another unsatisfactory goal. Pleasure or having good times is normally just an escape from the experience of discomfort. Too much pleasure in itself can become very dull. If life was all pleasure and nothing else, there would be no happiness.

Happiness has to do with being engaged. This is true in the workplace. This is also true away from the workplace. Being engaged literally means being totally immersed in any task. It means doing just one thing at a time, and enjoying it for all it's worth.

As they say in Zen, if you can't find it where you're standing, where do you expect to wander in search of it? The great minds of eastern philosphy have always said, "Happiness is the way." What they have been saying is happiness is not a destination. It is nothing you look for; you create it. You don't have to go looking for happiness .... if that's where you're coming from.

Humor Is No Laughing Matter

The ability to laugh is a great asset for living life to the fullest. The problem is most people think they possess a sense of humor, but few show it. The seriousness of some people I have met is enough to run complete trains off their rails.

In his early 90's George Burns started taking bookings for his 100th birthday. If he lives for more than a century, it will probably be because of the attitude he has carried throughout his life. He has made a living out of humor. Undoubtedly, his health has benefited from his work. Researchers are finding that boisterous laughing many times a day will give you the same effects as a ten-mile run.

> *"The most wasted day of all is that on which we have not laughed."*
>
> *- S.R.N. Chamfort*

Another man who benefited from laughter was Norman Cousins. Faced with what doctors diagnosed as a terminal illness, Cousins proved the medics wrong by watching reruns of Candid Camera and Groucho Marx films. He was able to laugh himself back to health.

Several years ago a group of high school students were given a test in creativity. Two equal sub-groups were formed. The first sub-group enjoyed the half hour before the test listening to a recording of a comedian. The other sub-group spent the half-hour in silence. The first sub-group did much better than the second group on the creativity test.

Besides being good for our health, humor is an effective way for promoting creativity. Experts in creativity have observed that stunning solutions are often triggered by humor. Seriousness hinders the creative flow. When you are under a lot of stress and pressure or stuck in a serious state of mind, the best thing to do is to get out a joke book. Get together with someone who can laugh about anything. Fool around. You'll be surprised at the many creative ideas which start to flow.

People who never get carried away should be. Most people have heard the saying, "Life is much too important to be taken seriously." Yet how many pay heed to this? Most are too serious. How serious are you in life? Do you find time to laugh, play, and be foolish? If you are always serious and trying to be reasonable, you are sabotaging your creativity. Individuals who are too serious to have fun rarely come up with new and stunning ideas about how to live life.

Play is at the heart of being creatively alive. Playing and having fun are great ways to stimulate our minds. When we are having fun, we tend to be relaxed and enthusiastic. Sometimes we even become outrageous. All these states complement the creative spirit.

Ever wonder why children are so creative? Children know how to be spontaneous, how to play, and how to have fun. Remember when you were a child. When you were playing, you were learning. You probably learned more during your lighter moments than during your serious moments. Try and re-experience the child in you if you want to increase your creativity. Keep the child in you alive and don't lose touch with the craziness in you. This will assure that your life will never be boring.

Comedy and laughing will open up your thinking. Laughing tends to make us look at things in unusual ways. This is because laughter changes our state of mind. In a relaxed state, our minds show little concern for being wrong or being practical. It is okay to be foolish; this fosters the flow of creative solutions. Creativity requires both playfulness and foolishness. These are the things society discourages. You may be told to "grow up", but you should never "grow up", because if you do, you will have stopped growing as an individual.

> *"Seriousness is the only refuge of the shallow."*
>
> *- Oscar Wilde*

If you are the serious type, learn to lighten up. As a friend once told me, "It is impossible to overestimate the unimportance of nearly everything."

The Ultimate Goal Is The Process

Free time and leisure time are not automatically rewarding. To create satisfaction in our lives, we must put in some effort and attain some accomplishment. If we want to achieve something significant, we must get the ball, get it rolling, and keep it rolling.

The happiest people in life are those who don't look for outside influences to make them happy. They are the ones who take action and make things happen. The doers of this world aren't content to just drift aimlessly and let life happen to them. They set goals and then take steps to attain them. The importance of setting goals was mentioned in Chapter 7. Once goals are set, working towards the goals is more important than attaining the goals.

Leo Tolstoy asked three questions:

(1) When is the best time to heed? Now.
(2) Who are the most esteemed people? He with whom you are.
(3) What important pursuits are to be undertaken first? That which does good to him.

When Leo Tolstoy answered these questions, he was reinforcing the power of being in the now. He was underscoring the importance of focusing on the process at hand, and not the end result. By focusing on the process, we get to enjoy both the process and the end result.

> *"The road is better than the inn."*
> *- Cervantes*

Living in the moment means there is more enjoyment and satisfaction from our efforts than from actually reaching the goal. Satisfaction from reaching a goal, no matter how significant the goal, is short lived. Robert Louis Stevenson said, "To travel hopefully is a better thing than to arrive." When the ultimate goal becomes the process, life is transformed. Creativity flows more readily, failure is viewed as success, and losing means winning; the journey becomes the destination.

To travel a happy journey, learn to cultivate a higher appreciation for what is around you - sunsets, music, and other beautiful things. Don't take things for granted because you'll miss life. Keep in mind that every sunset is different from all other sunsets, just like every snowflake is different from all other snowflakes. Wake up and listen to the birds sing, smell the flowers, and feel the texture of the trees.

Every second try to find something to enjoy. Look for the positive in all situations. Start and live each day with a task in mind. In your field of consciousness, practice the idea of enjoying your day. Act with a presence of mind and experience each moment by being in the now. Remember that there is no other moment than this one; you can live only one moment at a time. Ultimately you are the moment.

10. It Is Better To Be Alone Than In Bad Company

The Key To Being Alone Is Locked Inside

The Maytag man in television commercials is depicted as a lonely repairman. His services aren't required very often due to the high quality in Maytag appliances he is supposed to service. In one commercial the Maytag man registers at a hotel and signs his company name at the desk. The receptionist says something like, "We'll try to make sure you're not lonely here." In real life the receptionist would be fooling herself. No one can ever ensure the Maytag man isn't lonely except for the Maytag man himself. Furthermore, just because the Maytag man spends substantial time alone, he doesn't have to be lonely.

There are two sides to being alone: One side is the painful side which is loneliness. The other side to being alone is the pleasant side which is solitude. Discovering solitude can mean discovering many delightful activities which can only be enjoyed alone. Unfortunately, most people never discover the pleasant side to being alone.

> "A man who finds no satisfaction in himself, seeks for it in vain elsewhere."
>
> - La Rochefoucauld

To most people being alone means they experience the unpleasant side. I know people who can be driven off their rails if they are forced to be alone for more than ten minutes. Whenever these individuals wind up alone, they immediately are lonely.

Lonely people use aloneness as an excuse for not being able to do anything enjoyable in their spare time. I have a friend who was enthusiastic about cycling one summer. He bought a bicycle and then used it only once in the first two months. He wouldn't go cycling because he had no one with whom to cycle. I feel sorry for him, because he is missing out on great opportunities for enjoying his leisure. I often insist on going cycling or jogging alone, even when one or two friends are around and want to come along. Of course, I have to convince my friends that I don't find their company boring - merely I am looking for some solitude which I immensely treasure. There are times I prefer the pleasure I get from my own company.

I know other people who will put on the television and radio the minute they are alone. They will watch boring television programs, or listen to radio deejays engage in idle chatter, rather than deal with periods of silence. The inability to be alone is why many people remain in completely unfulfilling relationships rather than risk being alone.

It is most unfortunate that being alone is looked upon as antisocial behavior. Influenced by social programming, most people early in life learn to spend all their leisure time with planned social activities. They join clubs, teams, and any other organizations which will ensure they are with someone. If they wind up alone with unscheduled time on a long weekend, they are totally lost.

> *City Life: Millions of people being lonesome together."*
>
> *- Henry David Thoreau*

Psychologists say loneliness has become a serious problem in North America, especially in big cities. Surveys indicate one quarter of the population suffers from chronic loneliness. To some, loneliness is so painful they commit suicide. The following are some reasons people give for their loneliness:

× Not enough friends
× Not being married
× Not having a relationship
× Living in a new city
× Living in a big city
× Superficial friends

Loneliness is even more tragic considering no item in the above list ultimately causes loneliness. These may be influences but they don't cause loneliness. People become lonely because they allow themselves to get lonely. Loneliness reflects boredom.

To overcome boredom, we must learn how to spend time alone in a creative manner. The majority of us flee to society, as dull as society is, searching for some excitement to escape the greater dullness of ourselves. We also flee to society because we fear being alone. We feel we can avoid loneliness by being with people. However, we can be lonelier in a crowd than when we are alone.

If this is loneliness, I want more of it.

Loneliness isn't synonymous with aloneness. Feeling lonely isn't a result of living or being alone because being alone in itself will not make anybody lonely. The inability to be alone reflects some basic inner insecurity. Some of the loneliest people in the world are people who are always around other people. Many lonely people are extremely charming; they also appear to be self-confident and have great composure. Nevertheless, they are prone to loneliness the minute they are by themselves. Due to their lack of inner security, they spend every possible minute with other people.

The majority in society don't want to look inside themselves. Some take drugs or alcohol to keep the pace moving fast. Others, so they don't have to think, turn on the television or play the stereo to ensure there is always some sound during the times they are alone. The Sufi religious sect has a parable relating the folly of people looking to the external world for whatever they are searching. The parable is about their fictitious little man called Mullah.

One day Mullah is out on the street, outside his house, on his hands and knees looking for something. A friend happens to come by and says, "Mullah, what are you searching for?" The Mullah says, "I lost my keys." The friend says, "I'll help you look for them." After some time the friend finds looking for the keys quite tiresome and says to Mullah, "Mullah, do you have any idea where you lost the keys?" The Mullah replies, "Yes, I lost the keys in the house." The bewildered friend then asks the Mullah, "Why in the world are we looking for the keys outside?" Mullah

151

answers, "Because there is a lot more light out here."

This parable is funny, but it has a serious side to it. To handle loneliness, most people look to the external world where there is more light. Just as Mullah won't find his keys outside his house, people who look outside themselves to overcome loneliness won't find the key to handling loneliness. The key to handling loneliness and being alone is locked inside; loneliness can only be handled from the inside and not the outside. Once people recognize what causes their loneliness, being alone becomes an opportunity to do many interesting and enjoyable things, which they can't do around other people.

Enjoying Being Alone Takes High Self-Esteem

"If you can only make it with people, and not alone, you can't make it."

- Clark E. Moustakas

Being afraid to be alone is a sign of low self-esteem, and low self-esteem is a feeling of dislike for ourselves. This comes from a sense of feeling unworthy and undeserving. Our lives can feel like one big mess without self-esteem.

Many people are approval-seekers, always trying to get positive feedback from others. Even if it is forthcoming, this doesn't contribute to self-esteem. Esteem from others and self-esteem are two different things. As we saw in Maslow's hierarchy of needs, all of us would like esteem from others as well as from ourselves. The two esteem needs are not based on the same foundations.

In life there is no substitute for happiness, and there can be little happiness without self-esteem. Self-esteem cannot be achieved through other people and the environment; it is something individuals can only give themselves. People with low self-esteem are dependent upon how other people evaluate them. This makes them vulnerable to what others think or say. These other people are not the best judges, because they themselves probably have low self-esteem, and are caught up in trying to get approval from the achievement-oriented and money-making external world.

Can you enjoy being alone? If you can't, it is probably a sign that you are not able to discover quality in your own character. Not liking yourself can be a giant barrier to enjoyment from being alone in your leisure time. Incidentally, if you don't like yourself, why would you expect anyone else to like you?

Testing to what degree you like yourself involves looking at how much effort you put in trying to get others to like you. If you are constantly afraid someone may not like you, or may get upset with you, you probably have low self-esteem. On the other hand, if you have high self-esteem, you do not fear having people disagree with you, or even upset with you. As a person with high self-esteem, you undoubtedly have friends with quality, and not friends in quantity. There is a big difference here: Friends in quantity tend to be high in number, but superficial in character. Friends with quality are lower in number, but have greater character.

When I think about how modest I am about myself, I feel so proud.

Self-esteem is something you have to develop, if you lack it. It is based on your ability to like yourself no matter what others think about you. You may have to give up certain friends and acquaintances if they are not supportive in your transition. In doing so, you get to keep your own scorecard based on your own standards, rather than having someone keep your scorecard based on their standards.

You must love yourself and the world before you can serve the world. Developing higher self-esteem enables you to escape any rut in which you find yourself. Once you achieve higher self-esteem, you will learn how to accomplish, to achieve, and to triumph when alone. You will get to know yourself; in yourself is the universe.

Don't Just Walk Away From Negative People; RUN!

If you possess high self-esteem, you will avoid being around certain people, even if the alternative is being alone. While you are trying to light the fire in your life, learn to ignore those who will try to put it out for you. The boring person we talked about in Chapter 6 may douse it somewhat; even more dangerous to your happiness and well-being is the negative person.

Negative people are particularly noted for their lack of humor. They have this delightful view about how life is a ripoff. Nothing is so bad it can't get worse. Especially irritated by other people who are happy and highly motivated, they will do anything in their power to bring positive people down to their depressing level. At social gatherings these neurotics are the life of the party when they leave.

If you are the good-Samaritan type, who likes to take on one or two neurotics as a personal project, I must warn you about the futility of this venture. Unless you can get these people to have personality transplants, all your efforts will likely be in vain. Here is an old tale about a scorpion and a frog to put negative people in proper perspective:

> *"I will always cherish the initial misconceptions I had about you."*
>
> *- Unknown*

A scorpion, wanting to get across a pond, spots a friendly frog. The scorpion says to the frog, "How about a lift to the other side of the pond. I can't swim and I would appreciate your helping me out." The frog says, "No way. I know what scorpions are like. If I let you on my back, you'll probably sting me half way across the pond from where I could not swim to shore after being stung. I don't want to drown."

The scorpion replies, "Don't be silly. If I am on your back, I am dependent on you to get across the pond. If I sting you, not only will you drown, so will I. Why would I want to do that?" The frog thinks about this and relents, "I guess you're right, hop on." The scorpion hops on the frog's back and they take off for the other side of the pond. The scorpion resists stinging the frog until they are about half way across the pond. Then the scorpion who, like most of us, can resist everything but temptation, gives the frog a big whopper of a sting.

As both of them start to go under, the frog says to the scorpion, "Why in the world did you do that? Now both of us are going to die." The scorpion's answer is one you have heard many times before from human scorpions: "I couldn't resist it. It's my nature to be that way."

The moral behind this story is negative people will not change their nature even if their happiness and survival are at stake. Although they can change, negative people go on defending their point of view at all costs. Not only do they bring themselves down with their thinking, they try to bring others down with them. Misery doesn't only love company;

it demands it.

In dealing with negative people remember what Washington said: "It is better to be alone than in bad company." Based on my experiences, there is one way to effectively deal with negative people: Eliminate them from your life. I found using tear gas while I am wearing a gas mask to be most effective (just kidding again). The point is you should try and avoid negative people for the sake of your happiness. When you find yourself in their company, don't walk away from them; R U N !

Marital-Type Relationships Don't Cure Loneliness

Contrary to generally accepted but erroneous beliefs, single people without a marital-type relationship can be just as happy in life as someone who is happily married or involved in a relationship with another person. Often lonely people look to relationships and marriages to cure their loneliness. This seldom works. In many cases marriages and relationships actually complicate people's loneliness.

> *"Solitude makes us tougher towards ourselves and tenderer towards others: in both ways it improves our character."*
>
> *- Friedrich Nietzsche*

Exercise #10-1 - A Common Achievement

These great thinkers have been admired and acknowledged in Western history. They were regarded as generally happy and satisfied in life.

What did these great achievers have in common?

- ☆ Isaac Newton
- ☆ Friedrich Nietzsche
- ☆ Blaise Pascal
- ☆ Immanuel Kant
- ☆ John Locke

The above individuals made immense contributions to society. They also had something else in common: None of them ever married and most of them lived alone. Their happiness in this world wasn't dependent upon their being married.

In today's society, many people live alone. About nine percent of North Americans never marry; many others marry, but wind up single due to failed marriages or the death of spouses. Some people living alone are lonely; others are not.

Research at Ohio State University concludes it is a myth that loneliness is the result of living alone. A marriage certificate is not essential for a fulfilled life. Single people have more friends than do people in relationships, and well-adjusted singles are less troubled by headaches, anger, and irritability. Another research study confirms these findings. In interviewing never-married people between 58 and 94, two University of Guelph researchers, Joan Norris and Anne Martin Mathews, found the majority of singles are satisfied with their lives. People who stay single are known to develop strong friendships and have good jobs. Not being constrained by family obligations, they are able to experience joyful activities married people are not able to enjoy.

> *"All our evils come from not being able to be alone."*
>
> *- Jean de la Bruyere*

Marriage is not a cure for loneliness or low self-esteem. Many couples living together side by side are like two railroad tracks that run in the same direction, but never touch. Marriages like this can actually influence people to be lonelier and have lower self-esteem.

The stability in marriages has been undermined due to the exaggerated expectations people have from them. In his book, *Solitude: A Return To Self,* Anthony Storr makes the statement: "If we did not look to marriage as the principal source of happiness, fewer marriages would end in tears." Storr, a British psychiatrist, believes that interests, beyond relationships, help define healthy indentities and give meaning to lives. People need sources of fulfillment beyond their intimate relationships. According to Storr, what goes on in people's minds when they are alone is central to achieving fulfillment. The capacity to be alone reflects a basic security, which becomes increasingly important with the aging process.

Whether you are married, in a relationship, or single, it is a good thing to every so often separate yourself from people, newspapers, radio, and television for at least a day or two. Even if you don't have to spend much time alone at this time in your life, doing it is good for practice. The same reason applies for taking a sabbatical from work. If you do it now, you will be better prepared for it in the future if you are forced into it. Changes occur in our lives which alter the friendships and social structures we get used to. Retirement from work, moving to another city, or the death of someone close to us can create situations where we have to spend more time alone. Handling being alone prepares you for the times when you may not have as many people around you.

Flying Solo To Greater Heights

Enjoying being alone means making peace with yourself. If there is a key rule for getting the most from being alone, it is that you have to like and enjoy your own company. Being alone confronts you with yourself. You will find that being alone allows you to experience the world and yourself in a way not available when you are with other people. You get to fly solo rather than with someone else. By flying solo, you are able to achieve greater heights in your leisure pursuits.

My therapist told me that flying solo can be very rewarding. I wonder if she was pulling my leg.

The day you feel lonely you can react in one of two ways: One response is known as sad passivity. This includes crying, moping, excess eating, sleeping, and feeling sorry for yourself. This reaction comes from not having defined goals about what you can do alone. Undefined goals will mean you are flying solo too low. The only thing responsible for your loneliness is your inactivity. If you are the one who is inactive, you are the sole cause of your loneliness.

The other response is creative solitude where defined plans are used to best handle aloneness. This can include activities such as reading, writing letters, studying, listening to music, working on a hobby, or playing a musical instrument. When you start acting on your plans, you will enhance your identity and develop a sense of security.

Exercise #10-2 - Being Alone In Your Tree

Being alone is an opportunity to do the things which are difficult to do around other people. Go back to your leisure tree and add a primary branch for activities you can do alone. Now expand your tree by adding those activites which you can pursue alone.

Here are just a few of many things you can pursue without having someone by your side. Those which interest you are items you should add to your leisure tree under the category of doing things alone.

- ☐ Do some meditating and self-examination which is hard to do with other people
- ☐ Read books and magazines you haven't been able to read before
- ☐ Go visit people whom you may not visit when you are with another person
- ☐ Do something artistic or creative
- ☐ Try volunteer work
- ☐ Find time to dream your dreams
- ☐ Discover a new hobby
- ☐ Take up people watching
- ☐ Go to coffee places to meet people
- ☐ Cycle, jog, or swim
- ☐ Design a new tool or object
- ☐ Fix your car
- ☐ Remodel your house
- ☐ Go for a walk in the park
- ☐ Walk in the rain
- ☐ Take a nap
- ☐ Write letters
- ☐ Listen to music
- ☐ Study
- ☐ Play a musical instrument
- ☐ Work on a hobby
- ☐ Take up gardening
- ☐ Write a book

There are many more activities which can be pursued while alone. Overcoming loneliness when you are alone is dependent upon taking action and getting involved. Inactivity and isolation will lead to boredom and depression. Being alone provides you with an opportunity to develop your individuality, and to create quality in your leisure.

Peace of mind can be found in spending a night in your home and enjoying the quiet spaces. There is substance to being alone because it makes demands on your capacity to rely on yourself. More responsibility on your part is required when you are alone than when you are with a spouse, family, or friends. Taking responsibility means you get to be the author of your experiences, no matter what activity you happen to choose.

Solitude Is For The Sophisticated

While loneliness can mean dejection and sadness, solitude can mean contentment, and even ecstacy. Being alone and happy to be that way represents solitude. It is the sophisticated or the self-actualized personalities who treasure solitude. Self-actualized people are those at the highest level of self-development.

> *"Conversation enriches the understanding, but solitude is the school of genius."*
>
> *- Edward Gibbon*

Self-actualized people don't flee from aloneness; they seek it. In many leisure activities these people are at their best and most effective if they are alone. The self-actualized are centered - meaning they receive satisfaction in great measure from inside themselves because they appreciate solitude more than most people.

Note that the self-actualized are not loners who are always by themselves. Loners are people who don't get along with anyone; they are neurotic, secretly private, and poorly adjusted psychologically. In contrast, self-actualized individuals are psychologically healthy individuals who get along with most people. Abraham Maslow, the well-known humanist psychologist, found that these psychologically healthy individuals are highly independent, yet at the same time they enjoy people.

The paradox is that the people who are self-actualized appear to be loners. Although they may appear to be loners, they actually like to be with people and can be the most sociable. They are the most individualist members in society and at the same time are the most social, friendly, and loving. They have an ability to get along with others, but they also have the ability to get along with themselves. Consequently, self-directed people are free from the need to impress others, or to be liked by them.

Great! All the other leaves are gone. Now I can enjoy some solitude.

These creatively alive people have developed their natural ability - the ability which gives them the power to be happy in life. Because they have learned how to be independent, they have the ability to work alone and to play alone. The self-actualized do not base their identities on memberships in social groups. They can stand alone in their convictions and desires, often against the opinions and objections coming from others.

While self-actualized people enjoy the presence of others, they don't always need other people. Honors, prestige, and rewards are not as important for the mentally healthy. Not being as dependent on other people, they require less praise and affection.

If you want to ever attain self-actualization, it is imperative you enjoy being alone. Being self-actualized means you know that the quality in your inner life determines the quality in your external life. Your self-development and movement toward self-actualization can be wondrous, mysterious, and fascinating. Especially when you start spending substantial time alone, you will find a spiritual side to leisure. Quiet spaces will offer opportunity to reflect, to meditate, and to grow; you will find that Nirvana can be found at home in your own mind.

11. Being An Aristocrat On Less Than $20.00 A Day

Money May Not Be The Best Financial Security

This chapter is about money and what role money should play in our enjoyment of leisure time. Money plays a role, but not as big a role as the majority in our society believes.

Although most people don't know what it is they exactly want from life, they are absolutely sure that money in large amounts will provide it for them. The problem is that most people don't tell the truth about money. Money is more often misused and abused than used intelligently. People make many assumptions about money; most are terribly absurd.

One assumption people make about money is that money will guarantee their happiness. Money didn't guarantee a Montreal man's happiness. The *Vancouver Province* in 1990 reported on the plight of Jean-Guy Lavigueur, who in 1986 won a $7.6-million lottery. Lavigueur, unemployed at the time of his windfall, now lives with his girlfriend and her daughter in a 17-room mansion. That seemed to be the extent of the good news. The remaining news was that he never sees his daughter anymore, and many friends and relatives have deserted him because he wouldn't share his windfall with them.

> "Too many people are thinking of security instead of opportunity. They seem more afraid of life than death."
>
> - James F. Byrnes

Lavigueur stated, "I can buy what I want when I want it, but besides that I'm no more happy than anyone else...... you can't buy people. You either have friends or you don't. You can't buy love. You have to build love."

I could have cited many more cases such as this one. Many people acquire a large sum of money through hard work, inheritance, luck, or illegal means. Then they experience disappointment, and sometimes severe depression. North America has many affluent individuals who have all the material comforts they desire, yet lead lives of quiet and sometimes loud desperation. Experiencing a lingering pain, they understand that there is something missing; there is a big hole which needs to be filled. No matter how much exotic food and expensive wine they pour in the hole, and no matter what model of BMW, how big a house, and how much custom-designed furniture they stuff into the hole, the hole gets larger. As the hole gets larger, the pain becomes more unbearable.

> *"Poor and content is rich and rich enough."*
>
> *- Shakespeare*

Whether people are working or not working, money is a necessary commodity for their survival. Money is also a means for enhancing the ways in which they enjoy their leisure time. Unfortunately, where money is concerned, good sense ceases to exist. People look at money as an end, rather than as a means. Looking at money as an end in itself sets people up for great disappointment and dissatisfaction.

Exercise #11-1 - How Secure Are You?

Honestly answer these two questions: How much modern-day security do you expect in your life? How much money or how many material possessions do you think are necessary to lead a happy and fulfilling life?

Society has conditioned us to believe that we should be preoccupied with accumulating material wealth as security for our retirement and for the unexpected events in our lives. You will have problems with money if you start looking to money for total security. Just as you can't buy love and friends and family, you can't buy true security, despite the things the financial writers in your local newspapers have been telling you.

Security based on materialistic and monetary pursuits has many limits: The super rich can be killed in car accidents. Their health can fail just as easily as someone with much less money. War can break out and affect the rich as well as the poor. Many rich people worry about losing their money in the event the monetary system collapses.

Just because 20% of us in North America have 80% of the money, doesn't mean the rest of you have to be so grumpy about it.

Total security based on external possessions is another illusion in life. The people who are striving for security are among the most insecure, and the people who least care about security are the most secure. Emotionally insecure people seek to offset their unpleasant feelings by accumulating money in great measure as security against attacks on their egos. People striving for security by their very nature are very insecure. They depend on something outside themselves such as money, spouses, houses, cars, and prestige for security. If they lose all the things they have, they lose themselves, because they lose everything on which their identities were based.

It is interesting that the word "security" originally referred to internal - and only internal - security. "Security" is a derivative from the Latin word "securus" meaning "without care." A truly secure person has an internal security based on an inner creative essence.

If you have your health and the ability to care for yourself, the best security you can have is inner security. Security is the confidence to use your imagination to handle or overcome all the normal problems and situations that confront you as an individual. If you are a secure individual, you have learned how to be "without care." You don't spend much time focusing on financial security. The creative ability to always earn a living is the best financial security you can have. Your essence is based on who you are internally, and not on what you own. If you lose what you own, you still have your center of being; this allows you to carry on the normal process of living.

If Money Makes People Happy, Then Why......?

I like money for its intrinsic value, but I always make such a pig of myself with it.

Let's put money and its relationship to happiness in proper perspective. Money is an important element for our survival, but how much money we need to be happy is another matter. Hot-shot motivational speakers tell seminar participants that millionaires are winners. This implies that the rest of us are losers. Quite frankly, I can generate many reasons why most people with very modest means are more so winners in life than many millionaires we have read about in the newspapers lately.

Although money represents power, status, and safety in our society, there is nothing in its inherent nature to make us happy. To give youself a sense about the inherent nature of money, do the following exercise:

Exercise #11-2 - Will Money Love You?

Take out the money you have on you or around you at this time. Touch it and feel its warmth. Notice that it is fairly cold. It won't keep you warm at night. Talk to your money and see what happens. It won't respond. And no matter how much you love it, money won't love you in return.

Money is an expediency in life. To what degree money can enhance our lives depends more on how we intelligently use the money we have, than on how much we actually have. Michael Phillips, a former bank vice-president, thinks there are too many people whose identities are tied to money. In his book, *The Seven Laws of Money*, he discusses seven interesting money concepts:

> ⇨ Money has its own rules.
> ⇨ Money will come when you are doing the right thing for you.

⇨ Money is a dream - a fantasy as alluring as the Pied Piper.
⇨ Money is a nightmare.
⇨ You can never give money away as a gift.
⇨ You can never receive money as a gift.
⇨ There are worlds without money.

The uses for money are many. No one can challenge the important roles money plays in society and business, but anyone can challenge the myth that a large sum of money is synonymous with happiness. All one has to do is pay attention. Here are just a few significant observations I have made to the question:

> *"When a man says money can do anything, that settles it. He doesn't have any."*
>
> *- E.W. Howe*

If money makes people happy, then .....

♦ why did a recent survey indicate that a higher percentage of the people making over $75,000 a year are dissatisfied with their salaries than are people making less than $75,000 a year?

♦ why didn't Ivan Boesky, who illegally accumulated over $100 million through insider trading on Wall Street, stop his illegal actions after accumulating $2 million or $5 million but instead continued accumulating more millions until he got caught?

♦ why did members of a family I know (even though their financial net worth is in the top one percent for North American families), tell me how much happier they would be if they were to win a major lottery?

♦ why did a group of major lottery winners in New York form a self-help group to deal with post-lottery depression syndrome, a case of serious depression they had never experienced before winning their large sums of money?

♦ why do so many well paid baseball, football, and hockey players have drug and alcohol problems?

♦ why do doctors, one of the wealthiest groups of professionals, have one of the highest divorce, suicide, and alcoholism rates of all professionals?

♦ why do the poor give more to charities than the rich?

♦ why do so many rich people get in trouble with the law?

♦ why do so many wealthy people go to see psychiatrists and therapists?

> *"A million dollars doesn't always bring happiness. A man with ten million dollars is no happier than a man with nine million dollars."*
>
> *- Anon.*

The above are just a few warning signs that money doesn't guarantee happiness. As well as anyone else has been able to do, Benjamin Franklin expressed the folly in trying to achieve happiness through money. Franklin observed, "Money never made a man happy yet nor will it. There is nothing in its nature to produce happiness. The more a man has, the more he wants. Instead of its filling a vacuum, it makes one."

Exercise #11-3 - Which Is Easier To Come By?

Most people would like to be rich and happy. Which do you think is easier to acquire: a lot of money or happiness? (The answer is at the end of this chapter on page 174.)

I have a theory about how happy and emotionally "well-off" we will be with substantially more money than we have now. After we have satisfied our basic needs, money will neither make us happy nor unhappy. If we are happy and handle problems well when we are making $25,000 a year, then we will be happy and handle problems well when we have more money. If we are unhappy, neurotic, and don't handle problems well on $25,000 a year, then we can expect the same from ourselves with $1,000,000 a year. We will still be neurotics who are unhappy and can't handle our problems. The difference is we will be neurotics living with a lot more comfort and style.

Financial Independence On $6000 A Year

You don't have to be filthy rich to sit back and take it easy. As indicated in Chapter 1, the right attitude is important. With the right attitude, you can even live the life of Riley on borrowed money. By using an idea from Jerry Gillies' book, *Moneylove*, you can look at borrowed money as income. If this is too radical for you, because you want to live the life of Riley on your own money, then you must achieve financial independence. Achieving true financial independence so you can live a leisurely life may be easier than you think. It's not based on high finances.

> *"Let us all be happy and live within our means, even if we have to borrow to do it."*
>
> *- Artemus Ward*

An important factor for achieving financial independence is first defining what financial independence is. It may be possible to achieve financial independence without increasing your income or financial assets. All you have to do is change your concept concerning what financial independence is and what it isn't.

Exercise #11-4 - True Financial Independence

Which item from the list below is an essential factor for achieving financial independence?

- ☐   Winning a million-dollar lottery
- ☐   Having a good company pension complemented by a government pension
- ☐   Having inherited a bundle from wealthy relatives
- ☐   Being married to a rich spouse
- ☐   Having hired a financial consultant to help make the right investments

The results from a recent survey indicated, in order of importance, finance, health, and having a spouse or friends to share retirement were the biggest concerns for people just before retirement. What is interesting is that shortly after these people retired, health was considered the top priority and finances moved to third place. Apparently these people's concept of financial independence changed once they retired, although their expected income remained the same.

167

The results from this survey show that retired people can get by with much less than they first imagine. The survey also supports the notion that no item from the above list is a requirement for financial independence. The concept of true financial independence was clarified for me by my friend, Dan O'Brien, although I unconsciously had been living according to the concept for some time. Dan told me what he had learned about financial independence in a seminar presented by Joseph Dominguez. I later learned more about Dominguez from an article in the December, 1990 issue of the *New Age Journal.*

Joseph Dominguez is financially independent on an income which most people would claim is well below the poverty line. According to Dominguez, true financial independence can be achieved by many more people, if they are willing to do so. True financial independence is not to be confused with being a millionaire. Financial independence can be had on $500 a month or less. How? True financial independence is nothing more than having more money come in than goes out. If you are making $500 a month net and spending $499, you are financially independent.

> *"Taking it all in, I find it is more trouble to watch after money than to get it."*
>
> *- Montaigne*

What Dominguez has done for years is live on $500 a month. In 1969, at the age of 29, he retired financially independent. Before he retired, Dominguez was a stockbrocker on Wall Street. He was appalled to see many unhappy people who were living at high socioeconomic levels.

Eventually Dominguez decided he didn't want to work in this environment, so he designed a personal financial program based on a simplified lifestyle. His lifestyle is comfortable, but only costs $6000 a year, which comes from his investments in US Treasury bonds made with money he had saved. Because his needs are so few, he has been able to donate all the extra money he has made since 1980 from his public seminar, *Transforming Your Relationship with Money and Achieving Financial Independence,* to nonprofit organizations.

Our material needs aren't many; the needs can be limited to food, water, and some shelter from the elements. In North America most people live in luxury, but don't realize it. More than two changes of clothes can be a luxury. Owning a house is a luxury. A television is a luxury. A car is a luxury. Many people will scream that these are necessities, but they aren't. I know many people who don't own either a car or a television or a house and are living quite well.

I am not saying everyone should cut back to the bare essentials. Although I have over the last few years had an income that at times was below the poverty line, there are some luxuries in my life I have maintained and would rather not give up. The point is that most people can cut back at least some expenses. Many luxuries bring people essentially nothing but falsely inflated egos. Conspicuous consumption to display luxury is an attempt to prove superiority by flaunting wealth - bigger houses than one needs, cellular phones, expensive cars, and the latest stereos - in the face of others, mainly the less wealthy. This behavior shows a lack of essence and self-esteem.

With just a little more prudence in spending, most people can cut their expenses substantially. It is amazing how little people need when they use some creativity and resourcefulness. Hopefully the shop-till-you-drop mentality prevalent in the 1980's will fade away in the 1990's and be replaced by some sanity. In the 1980's people lost their intrinsic values. They bought things, many which were nothing short of junk, to impress their friends.

There are signs more North Americans in this decade are seeking a slower pace and the smaller pleasures in life. For example, when I was writing this chapter, I read about a truly financially independent, but not wealthy, family enjoying a slower pace and the smaller pleasures. The *Edmonton Journal* on July 16, 1991 reported on Brent and Dolores Andressen who live in St. Albert, Alberta. They are doing just fine living on about one half of an income. Although both are trained school teachers, who could be collectively earning over $100,000 a year, Brent is the only one who works, and part time at that. Brent and Delores have two young daughters and are able to live comfortably on less than $30,000 a year. By cutting back expenses, the Andressens have achieved financial independence.

> *"Goodness is the only investment that never fails."*
>
> *- Henry David Thoreau*

The Andressens have lived simply for the last decade; they say there has been no hardship at all. They feel good about themselves because they are doing their part to conserve the environment. In fact, their philosophy has become "less is more." With a lower income, Brent and Dolores have managed to buy a precious commodity which many people with ten times their income haven't been able to buy. The precious commodity is the substantial amount of leisure time in which they can do what they want to do.

A Theory To Work With Or Play With

"Money doesn't buy happiness, but it pays for the illusion that it does."

- Anon

The foundations for being happy at leisure are not much different than those for being happy at work. Much of what constitutes happiness has to do with satisfaction. Money has nothing to do with the attainment of satisfaction at either work or leisure. Satisfaction is determined by how motivated we are and how much we achieve at our activities.

Another motivational theory almost as popular as Maslow's Theory of the Hierarchy of Needs is one called the "Two-Factor Theory" developed by Frederick Herzberg. Like Maslow's theory, Herzberg's Two-Factor Theory has been applied to studying what motivates employees in the workplace. Herzberg never applied his theory to leisure; however, I am going to do it for him because his principles are equally applicable to leisure.

After interviewing many workers in several different industries, Herzberg found that the work characteristics associated with dissatisfaction were quite different from those pertaining to satisfaction. This prompted the notion that there are two significantly different classes of factors affecting motivation and job satisfaction.

As indicated in Figure #11-1, there is a neutral point on the scale where individuals are neither satisfied nor dissatisfied. What will get people dissatisfied is the lack of hygiene factors - adequate wages, job security, working conditions, and status. If the hygiene factors are adequately provided, they will not in themselves result in employee satisfaction. Only a neutral state - no dissatisfaction - will have been attained.

If people are to have job satisfaction, the motivational factors - recognition, achievement, personal growth, and responsibility - must be provided. These are called motivators because they are concerned

170

Figure #11-1 - Herzberg's Two-Factor Theory

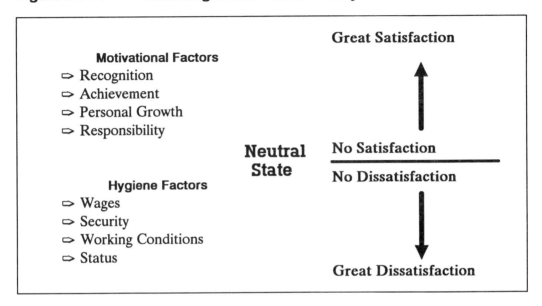

Motivational Factors
⇨ Recognition
⇨ Achievement
⇨ Personal Growth
⇨ Responsibility

Hygiene Factors
⇨ Wages
⇨ Security
⇨ Working Conditions
⇨ Status

Great Satisfaction

Neutral State

No Satisfaction

No Dissatisfaction

Great Dissatisfaction

about the work itself and, therefore, are effective in creating job satisfaction which leads to greater performance and productivity.

Let's get back to money. In the workplace money is important for eliminating dissatisfaction. For an unemployed carpenter, who is broke and doesn't have a place to live, money is very important. Getting the money to rent a basic one-bedroom apartment will go a long way to make her life more comfortable. However, once she has enough money to get a basic place to live, getting more money from her job - even enough to buy a 117-room mansion - is not going to do anything towards contributing to more happiness and satisfaction at the job. Her dissatisfaction will have been eliminated to a point where she is neutral. Unless she gets some motivators in her job, no matter how much she is paid, she will not attain satisfaction and happiness from her work.

The same principles of Herzberg's theory apply to our leisure time. Money is a hygiene factor which will take care of only so much. Without any motivators in place, the most we can hope for, even with a billion dollars to spend on our leisure, is to get to the neutral state of no dissatisfaction. If we want to create the conditions for satisfaction in our leisure, we must incorporate at least one or two motivators in our activities.

An important ingredient for happiness and satisfaction in life is the opportunity to complete difficult tasks. The more difficult and challenging the task, the more satisfaction we will get from completing the task. For example, one thing people find extremely difficult is to quit smoking. Many people who have quit smoking will say it was the most difficult thing they have ever done. At the same time, they will tell you that of anything they have done in their lives, giving up smoking gave them the most satisfaction, mainly because it was such a challenging and arduous accomplishment.

Of all the ways I have tried to get recognition, this one has to be the most creative and the most absurd.

A difficult task for me was writing and self-publishing my first book. Self-publishing the book was a great challenge because major publishers told me there was no market for the book. To complicate the situation, I had no experience in publishing and marketing books. I even had to borrow money if I wanted to publish it myself. Nevertheless, I took the risk and published it. The book has been a great success; it is in the top ten percent of non-fiction books ever sold in North America. Because I was willing to risk and do the difficult and uncomfortable, my life became a lot easier. What I did was incorporate motivators - achievement, responsibility, growth, and recognition - into the activity of publishing my book. I ended up experiencing satisfaction to a great degree from what was a significant personal accomplishment.

If you want to get satisfaction in great measure from your leisure pursuits, ensure you are involved in activities with Herzberg's motivational factors in place. Choosing an inexpensive activity, such as volunteering for a charitable organization, can bring you more happiness than spending $5000 on a new wardrobe. Helping others while working for a charity puts in place achievement, responsibility, growth, and recognition. The result is satisfaction on a large scale which no amount of money can ever buy.

Inexpensive Activities Fit For Royalty

Most North Americans have been conditioned to believe leisure is something that only money can provide. Much of what Madison Avenue wants us to do in our spare time is based on conspicuous consumption; it requires that we own a financial gravy train which doesn't lose any locomotion. Creating more spare time is encouraged only for the purpose of buying more products and services. Excessive emphasis on acquiring money and material things will not bring security. Many things that matter the most don't require much money. In fact, some of the best things in life are free!

> *"A happy heart is better than a full purse."*
>
> *- Italian Proverb*

John Stuart Mill predicted more than a hundred years ago that if the world continued on its path of economic growth, the environment would be totally destroyed. His premise was that wealth, as defined by western nations, is dependent upon defacing the environment. As some of us are now aware, the environment cannot withstand the demands we have increasingly placed on it.

Our addiction to excessive materialism to keep us busy and make us successful must be cured. Most economists and business people see leisure as positive only if we have money and it leads us to buy more leisure items and services. Money has its limitations, as indicated by John Kenneth Galbraith, the well-known economist, who views money and consumption in a different light than do most economists.

"I am not quite sure what the advantage is in having a few more dollars to spend if the air is too dirty to breathe, the water too polluted to drink, the commuters are losing out in the struggle to get in and out of the city, the streets are filthy and the schools so bad that the young perhaps wisely stay away, and the hoodlums roll citizens for some of the dollars they saved in the tax cut."

Enjoyable leisure is not what advertisers are trying to sell us. Vacations, for example, don't require much money. You don't have to get away to have a get-away vacation. Before venturing across the world in search of greener grass, check out the wonder of the world in your own back yard. Sometimes the grass is greener on our side of the fence. I am not saying you shouldn't see the world. What I am saying is that it isn't necessary to travel to exotic locales to enjoy yourself.

Leisure goals don't have to be hard on the pocket book or on the environment. Keep in mind that the activities most environmentally friendly are ones which cost us the least money. Watching sunsets, going for walks, meditating, having interesting conversations, wading through streams, and exercising in the parks are activities which cost us virtually nothing and help preserve the environment. These inexpensive activities are also enjoyable enough to be fit for royalty.

In a materialistically oriented world, simple pleasures are easily forgotten. Quality leisure is much more than spending big money on activities such as staying in expensive hotels, going on exotic tours, and shopping in exclusive boutiques. In fact, the less we need, the freer we become. Simple lifestyles can become pleasures in themselves. One way to become rich is to pay attention to what we already have. The Buddhists say, "Want what you have and you will always get what you want." Most of us have forgotten about the many riches we have. Many people in third world countries would view these as treasures. Books, music, old friends, neglected hobbies, and favorite pastimes are waiting to be rediscovered, if only we are willing to overcome our blindness.

> *"That man is the richest whose pleasures are the cheapest."*
>
> *- Thoreau*

Don't base your ability to indulge in leisure pursuits on money alone. More security can come from challenging and refining your beliefs and values than from saving money in great amounts. By developing your interests and hobbies, and enhancing the quality in your leisure activities, you will be on your way to having more security than many millionaires. No matter how much money you possess, you can have even greater wealth for enjoying leisure: The wealth is your talent, knowledge, experience, and creative ability.

Answer to Exercise #11-3 - Money would appear easier to come by than happiness; this is based on the observation that there are no happy neurotics, but there are many rich ones.

12. The End Has Just Begun

It's Not Over Until It's Over

You may have noticed that this is the last chapter, which signifies the end of the book. It may look like the end, but the end has just begun. Yogi Berra made a powerful statement about a baseball game: "It's not over until it's over." This is how you should look at your life, no matter how old you are, or to what age you live. As a reader of this book, you may be in your early teens or over a hundred years old. Regardless of your age, you should avoid being like many people who are living life as though it was over, many years before it's actually over.

There is a story about an 85-year-old woman who goes to the doctor with an ailment in her right knee. The doctor examines the knee and then states, "Really Mrs. Jones, what do you expect? It is after all an 85-year-old knee." Not to be swayed by this doctor's preconceived notions about the effects of aging, Mrs. Jones replies, "I beg to differ, Doctor Jensen. The knee may certainly be 85, but this can't be the cause of my problem. My left knee is also an 85-year-old knee, and it's just fine."

> "Here is a test to find whether your mission on earth is finished:
> If you're alive, it isn't."
> - From *Illusions* by Richard Bach

The point of this story is that all of us, even doctors, can have preconceived notions about how age affects us as we grow older. A Chinese proverb states, "Man fools himself. He prays for a long life and fears old age." Erroneous beliefs about old age can become self-fulfilling prophecies. If we allow ourselves to be influenced by ageism, we will come up with excuses for not pursuing those activities which we can pursue well into our 80's, 90's, and beyond. Old age will be feared if we retreat from life. Taking a new approach to life, rather than retreating from it, is the key to enjoying our later years. No matter what age we are and how close we think we are to the end, we should always look at new opportunities for personal growth, achievement, and satisfaction.

Being over the hill means picking up speed.

The August, 1989 issue of the magazine, *The Writer,* reported a 95-year-old Worcester, Massachusetts former newspaper columnist, Jane Goyer, had just sold her first book for publication to Harper & Row Publishers. One Harper & Row editor was quoted as saying, "She wasn't signed up because she's 95 ... but because she's an excellent writer with an unusual perspective who has something new to say." Harper & Row thought this "new" 95-year-old writer showed so much promise that they asked her to agree to an option on her second book. The editor went on to say, "I'm partial to authors who are good investments for the future."

Jane Goyer has shown that youngsters have not cornered the market on accomplishment. Creative and energetic living is not restricted to those with youth and excess energy. Here are a few more examples of people who have lived active lifestyles in their later years:

* At 94 Bertrand Russell was actively promoting international world peace.
* Mother Teresa, now 80, is as active as she has ever been in helping the poor through her Missionaries of Charity.
* At 90 Picasso was still active in creating drawings and engravings.
* Linus Pauling, a two-time Nobel laureate for chemistry and peace, is active at 90 looking for new ways to justify us taking megadoses of vitamins.
* Luella Tyra was 92 in 1984 when she competed in five categories at the United States Swimming Nationals in Mission Viejo, California.

* Lloyd Lambert at 87 is an active skier and running a 70+ Ski Club which has 3,286 members including a 97-year-old.
* Maggie Kuhn, at 83, is still active in promoting the goals of the Grey Panthers, a seniors group which she helped found when she was 65.
* Buckminister Fuller in his 80's was actively promoting his vision for a new world.
* Harvey Hunter of Edmonton recently celebrated his 104th birthday. (When asked about the secret for a long life, he replied, "Keep breathing.") Harvey became a volunteer when he was 90 and started university at 91. He still volunteers one day a week.

These people appear to be somewhat remarkable, and in a way they are. Nevertheless, they are not unusual. Hundreds of thousands of people in their 70's, 80's, and 90's have an incredible zest for life and show great vigor, enthusiasm, and physical ability in living. To some seniors, being over the hill means picking up speed.

Why Creatively Alive Individuals Don't Need A Second Childhood

After I wrote a magazine article on how people can be creatively alive in their later years, I received several calls from readers. One caller was June Robertson who was six months away from her 90th birthday. The enthusiasm and energy that she expressed on the telephone was overwhelming. I know people in their 20's and 30's who probably haven't shown that much enthusiasm and energy for more than one minute in their lives.

I learned some very interesting things about June. After her husband passed away many years ago, she never married again. Her income has been below the poverty line on occasion. Yet she has managed to travel to Russia, Africa, Europe, and India, as well as several other countries. Unfortunately, she had to cancel a visit to China when she became ill, but she still intends to go at a later date.

> *"When I grow up I want to be a little boy."*
> - Joseph Heller

June became a public speaker in her 70's. She didn't know she could do it until she appeared as a guest on a radio open line show. The people at the radio station liked her so much that they asked her to take over the show for a week. She was paid $20 a day and enjoyed it immensely. She would have done it for nothing. Showing her love for adventure, June went up in a hot air balloon when she was 78.

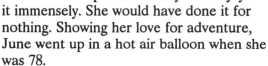

By doing nothing today, I, in fact, will be doing something.

Yes Sam, you will be creating more paradox in your life.

All you television junkies, take heed! When I mentioned televison to June, she told me that she watches very little TV and called it the "dumb box." Incidentally, she does have an addiction; it is books. I would say that if anyone is going to have an addiction, this is a rather good one to have.

When I asked June what advice she would give to us on how to live life to the fullest as we get older, she said first we must not let our spirits down. (Note this relates to attitude, the first thing stressed in this book.) Then she added, "We also must live gloriously, happily, and dangerously."

Seniors like June Robertson, who live life to the fullest, have this enlightened awareness about how much alive they really are. They have developed certain character traits which really stand out.

Exercise #12-1 - Prime Qualities

Spend two or three minutes thinking about individuals who are in their sixties or older and are still vibrant, active, and enjoying life to the fullest. List the qualities which these people have.

One of the most precious traits which seniors with a zest for life have is their continuing wonder with life - the ability to enjoy each new rainbow, sunset, and full moon. Here are some other qualities that participants in my seminars list for the active and vibrant seniors whom they know:

⇨ creative
⇨ spontaneous
⇨ sense of humor
⇨ playful
⇨ energetic
⇨ friendly
⇨ inquisitive
⇨ laughing
⇨ crazy
⇨ ability to act foolish
⇨ adventurous
⇨ adaptive
⇨ joyful

Exercise #12-2 - Who Else Qualifies?

What age group other than that of seniors has most or all of the above qualities?

Of course, the other age group with these qualities is that of children. Creatively alive seniors are like children in many ways. They easily adapt to changing circumstances as required. Being adventurous optimists, they are always willing to take up new activities such as playing an instrument, public speaking, tennis, or windsurfing. Seniors with a remarkable zest for life make an effort to totally experience each and every single moment. Like young children, they get into the moment unselfconsciously and become fully absorbed in it to the exclusion of everything else. Creatively alive adults know how to play, laugh, be spontaneous, and express their joy at being alive. People, who are active and happy in their later years, don't need a second childhood because they never gave up their first.

> *"The only truly happy people are children and the creative minority."*
>
> *- Jean Caldwell*

The Inner World Of Leisure

Although maintaining our child-like traits is important for successful aging, our leisure pursuits should go beyond the external world as we grow older. Trying to maintain our youth is not what growing older is all about. Over time our physical fitness will gradually decline, no matter how much effort we put into being fit. However, our minds can continue to grow, and become gradually more fit with time. Continued personal growth contributes to a more fulfilling life due to the increased wisdom and richness we acquire with age.

As you approach or enter your senior years, the concept of retirement first enters the picture. Don't ever actually commit yourself to retirement; it should not be taken literally. For those who take retirement literally, death comes much faster because they end up sitting idly around the house. Retirement should be a reorientation of living. We should call the disengagement from a job self-actualization or self-realization rather than retirement. Either term would signify that we are soaring to new heights, both outwardly and inwardly, in our later years.

Again, it is worthwhile to mention Morris M. Schnore's extensive research study at the University of Western Ontario (first mentioned in Chapter 5). Schnore found that a healthy adjustment to retirement was not based on being healthy, wealthy, and highly educated as previously thought. Although health was important, income and high education were not significant in determining happiness in retirement. Low expectations, positive evaluation of one's situation, self-competence, and internal orientation were found to be the most important contributors to satisfaction in people's retirement.

> *"Grow old along with me!*
> *The best is yet to be."*
> *- Robert Browning*

Commitment towards developing an inner orientation is the foundation for an inner world in leisure. Internal orientation may not sound important to individuals in their teens or early twenties, but this is an essential ingredient for self-development as we grow older. This relates to the spiritual self, and is the element in the wheel of life (shown on page 54) which is most neglected, ignored, or denied by people in our materialistically oriented society. The spiritual self is attained through much higher levels of consciousness than those used in sports, entertainment, or working. Communicating with the inner higher self can be reason enough to live a long life.

Committing yourself to the inner life and the voice within will result in strength and confidence not available in the outer world. Losing contact with the higher self can result in despair and depression in your mature years. The way to escape loneliness and despair is to tune into the spiritual world, which will help you enhance your internal essence. Self-development can be mysterious, but it is also wondrous and fascinating. Self-questioning results in self-determination which results in great freedom. Realizing your higher self will make you a much more creative and dynamic individual. Your life will be a joy to behold, because it has richness and quality.

> *"For the ignorant, old age is as winter; for the learned, it is a harvest.*
> *- Jewish Proverb*

Walking The Talk Instead Of Talking The Walk

Throughout this book I have emphasized many principles for achieving satisfaction in leisure. Here for your review are the most important principles:

* How's your attitude today?
* Don't walk away from negative people; run!
* Keep focused on your needs and your goals
* Are you paying attention?
* Satisfy three important needs: structure, purpose, and community
* Create a leisure tree
* Have a balance between active and passive activities
* Money will not make you happy or unhappy
* Always remember the Easy Rule Of Life
* Generate many ideas for living
* Strive for personal growth, recognition, responsibility, and achievement
* If you are bored, remember who is causing it
* Don't miss the moment; master it
* The ultimate goal is the process

I'm getting pretty good at this. Maybe I should give other people sleeping lessons.

* Be spontaneous
* Dare to be different
* Risk
* Solitude is for secure people
* Laugh and be silly
* The best things in life are free
* Keep physically fit
* Take part in eclectic activities
* Avoid excessive TV watching
* Keep mentally fit
* Goof off at times
* Develop the inner world of spiritual essence

Having developed skills for leisure won't guarantee that you will gain satisfaction from leisure just as owning a horse won't guarantee you will ride the horse and appreciate it. You have to motivate yourself in some way to do what is necessary to attain satisfaction at anything worth doing.

It is one thing to acknowledge problems in life and decide what must be done to change. Most people can reach this point. Where most people fail is in doing something about it. Inaction renders the knowledge of the problem and what to do about it worthless.

There is an old saying, "talk is cheap because supply exceeds demand." Many people talk about the many wonderful things they are going to do in life, but never get around to doing very many of them. Talking about the walk is one thing; walking the talk is another issue altogether.

"After all is said and done, more is said than done."

- Anonymous

Walking the talk is about commitment. Many people use the word commitment but they don't really know what it means. Using the word, because it sounds nice, does not represent commitment. The majority say they are committed to being happy and successful in life. Their actions represent the opposite of commitment. When they learn their goal requires time, energy, and sacrifice, they give up the goal.

Here is a simple test to determine how committed you are to your goals and making your life work: Do you do the things you say you are going to do? This applies to seemingly insignificant items like calling a person when you say you will. If you are not doing the small things that you say you will, I have a hard time believing you will be committed to larger goals. If commitment is lacking in your life, you won't attain very much satisfaction in the long run.

> *"There is nothing brilliant nor outstanding in my record, except perhaps this one thing: I do the things that I believe ought to be done .... And when I make up my mind to do a thing, I act."*
>
> *- Theodore Roosevelt*

Your actions are the only thing that will attest to your commitment. A seriousness about commitment will mean you have the intense desire to achieve your goals, no matter what barrier or wall appears in your way. If a wall appears in the way of your goals, you will try to go over or under or through the wall. If this doesn't work, you can go to the left or to the right. If you still aren't successful, you will try blowing up the wall or burning it. Then again, you can always move it.

Leisure provides unlimited opportunities for growth and satisfaction. There is no reason to wind up bored if you are committed to your happiness. So when you find yourself away from the workplace, commit yourself to what has to be done. If after reading this book you still find yourself with too much spare time, then try:

- ☞ Walking to the store rather than driving your car
- ☞ Helping others instead of having others help you
- ☞ Experiencing a sunset for 15 minutes rather than glancing at it
- ☞ Learning to spend more time alone so you get to experience the pleasures from solitude
- ☞ Reading a good book instead of watching TV
- ☞ Undertaking challenging activities instead of easy ones
- ☞ Finding someone interesting to talk to - someone who is sometimes going to question or disagree with the things you believe in
- ☞ Throwing a party for many interesting people (Don't forget to invite me)

As you sow, so shall you reap. In other words, whatever you put in the universe will be reflected back to you. It takes action - plenty of it - to get fulfillment and satisfaction in your life. Don't be like most people who don't follow through with action. Your positive attitude and enthusiasm for living are the ingredients for being committed to action, and a life that works. When it comes to commitment, always remember these words of wisdom from the Buddhists: "To know and not to do is not yet to know."

Life Begins At Your Leisure

It is my wish that something in this book will have helped you to spend your spare time with as much enjoyment and fulfillment as I have experienced from writing this book. I trust that the process of enhancing your leisure time has already begun for you; just having read this book is a significant accomplishment in itself.

> *"I wish I'd drunk more champagne."*
>
> *- Last words of John Maynard Keynes, Economist*

Now you must do something with what you have learned. Activity and inner mobility will go a long way. You have to love the world to be of service to it. Always try to seek growth, not perfection. You are the creator of the context in which you view things. It is up to you to find a way to enjoy the activities you undertake. Your task is to fill up any idle time, so that anxiety, boredom, and depression have no place in your world of leisure. Let your interests be as wide as possible; the variety in life makes the effort to experience that variety well worthwhile.

When you are feeling no zest for life, find a way to turn on your enthusiasm fast. Routine and the need for security can imprison you to a life with indifference and boredom. Try to deliberately seek new pursuits, just to keep some freshness and excitement flowing. Court the unexpected; invite new people and events into your daily life. Take more chances and risks. Learn to enjoy interesting people, interesting food, interesting places, interesing culture, and interesting books.

I must also emphasize simplicity. Remember that the greatest pleasures don't necessarily come from spectacular events or incredible moments. Intense pleasure can come from many basic things in life.

You don't really have to seek happiness in your leisure time. Three gifts were given to you when you were born: the gift of love, the gift of laughter, and the gift of life. Use these gifts and happiness will follow you wherever you go.

Keep in mind that attitude is the most important element. By shaping your own attitude, you make life what it is. No one but you gets to make your own bed. No one but you can ever put in the effort to make your life work. No one but you can generate the joy, the enthusiasm, or the motivation to live your life to the fullest.

> *"You only live once. But if you work it right, once is enough."*
>
> *- Fred Allen*

Leisure is a treasure to cherish and cultivate at all stages in your life. If you still haven't realized how precious leisure really is, here is something you should consider: How many people have you heard about who on their death bed said, "I wish I would have worked more." I bet you haven't heard about very many. In all probability, if there is anything you are going to regret not having done in your life, it will be something you could have done in your leisure and not at work. There is a good reason for this: The most precious moments you will experience are those coming from the joy of not working.

Your life begins at your leisure ...... bon voyage!

If you have enjoyed the book and have any thoughts, comments, or experiences that you would like to let me know about, I would be happy to hear from you. Address all letters to:

Ernie Zelinski
P.O. Box 4072
Edmonton, Alberta
Canada, T6E 4S8

Bibliography And Recommended Reading

Juliet B. Schor's *The Overworked American* (BasicBooks, 1991)

Faith Popcorn's *The Popcorn Report* (Doubleday, 1991)

Barbara Killinger's *Workaholics: The Respectable Addicts* (Key Porter, 1991)

Dr. Herbert J. Freudenberger's and Geraldine Richelson's *Burn Out: How To Beat The High Cost Of Success* (Bantam Books, 1980)

Anne Wilson Scheaf's *When Society Becomes An Addict* (Harper & Row, 1987)

Anne Wilson Scheaf's and Diane Fassel's *The Addictive Organization* (Harper & Row, 1988)

Diane Fassel's *Working Ourselves To Death: The High Cost Of Workaholism And The Rewards Of Recovery* (Harper, 1990)

Richard Bach's *Illusions: The Adventures Of A Reluctant Messiah* (Dell, 1977)

Jerry LeBlanc's & Rena Dictor LeBlanc's *Suddenly Rich* (Prentice-Hall, 1978)

Morris M. Schnore's *Retirement: Bane or Blessing* (Wilfrid Laurier University Press, 1985)

Peter Hanson's *The Joy Of Stress* (Hanson Stress Management Org., 1985)

Jerry Gillies' *Money-Love* (Warner Books, 1978)

Herb Goldberg's and Robert R. Lewis' *Money Madness* (Signet Books, 1978)

Shakti Gwain's *Living In The Light* (Whatever Publishing, 1986)

Roger von Oech's *A Whack On The Side Of The Head* (Warner Books, 1983)

John Naisbitt's and Patricia Aburdene's *Megatrends 2000* (William Morrow & Co., 1990)

Anthony Storr's *Solitude: A Return To Self* (Collier Macmillan, 1988)

Erich Fromm's *To Have Or To Be* (Bantam, 1976)

Dennis Wholey's *Are You Happy* (Houghton Mifflin Company, 1986)

Antoine de Saint Exupery's *The Little Prince* (Harcourt, Brace, Jovanocich, Inc., 1943)

Bertrand Russell's essay, *In Praise Of Idleness* (found in Robert Camber's & Carlyle King's *A Book Of Essays*, Gage Educational Publishing, 1963)

Ken Dychtwald's *Age Wave* (J. P. Tarcher Inc., 1989)

About The Author

Ernie Zelinski is a consultant specializing in applying creativity to both business and leisure. As a professional speaker, he has spoken to audiences at many conferences and management retreats hosted by organizations such as the Canadian Association of Pre-Retirement Planners, Canadian Association of Insurance Women, Canadian Trucking Association, the Saskatchewan Public Service Commission, Junior Achievement, Greater Edmonton Teachers' Convention Association and the Calgary Teacher's Convention Association.

Ernie's first book, *"The Art Of Seeing Double Or Better In Business"*, is about how all of us can be more innovative. Besides being the author of two books, he has written many articles on creativity and leisure, which have appeared in American and Canadian publications such as Teaching Today Magazine, Human Resource Magazine, Vancouver Business Examiner, London Business Monthly, and Training Magazine.

Ernie has an Engineering degree and a Masters in Business Administration. As a part-time instructor in business, he has taught his principles of creativity to students at the University of Alberta and Grant MacEwan College in Edmonton, and Simon Fraser University and City University in Vancouver.

Ernie lives in Edmonton and spends as much time as he can in Vancouver, which he considers his second home. He has been 35 years old for the last eight years, because he likes the age 35. Cycling and tennis are his two favorite sports. Although he does not own a motorcycle, Ernie is a member of the Lemmings Motorcycle Club. He watches television about once a month. He reads every day and prefers non-fiction over fiction. He has leisurely started writing his third book which he plans to complete some time in the near or distant future.

Speeches & Seminars By Ernie Zelinski

   Let Ernie Zelinski custom design a seminar or keynote speech for your next convention, meeting, management retreat, or company sponsored cruise. These are his popular topics:

- **"The Joy Of Not Working"**

  How individuals can enhance their lives with quality leisure.

- **"Creative Leisure Just For The Health Of It"**

  How employees can create a more balanced lifestyle.

- **"Thinking Way Out In Left Field"**

  How individuals can be more creative in the workplace.

- **"Management And Leadership For Innovation"**

  How managers can lead organizations to be more innovative.

   You can book Ernie Zelinski for a speech or workshop by writing or calling:

Pauline Price or Linda Davidson
Can*Speak Presentations
North Vancouver, BC, V7L 1V3
Phone (604) 986-6887
Toll Free Number (In Canada)
Phone (800) 665-7376

Ernie Zelinski
Visions International Publishing
P.O. Box 4072
Edmonton, Alberta
Canada, T6E 4S8
Phone (403) 436-1798

The Art Of Seeing Double Or Better In Business

How All Of Us Can Be More Innovative

In *The Art Of Seeing Double Or Better In Business*, Ernie Zelinski invites you on a journey of learning. You will discover how to be more innovative in business and your personal life. Blending humor, practical examples, numerous illustrations, and entertaining exercises, the author uses a style which appeals to readers from all walks of life.

This book was selected as an Editor's Choice by New York's *Success* Magazine. Since then American and Canadian organizations have been buying the book to enhance business performance of staff and clients. Hundreds of school teachers have also purchased the book as a resource for teaching creativity in the classroom.

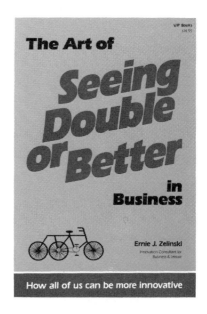

To order single copies on your credit card by telephone: Call toll free 1-800-265-4559 in Canada and 1-800-356-9315 in USA

To order <u>autographed</u> copies of *"The Art Of Seeing Double Or Better In Business"* by mail, send $19.95 per book (includes postage, handling, and tax). Send $14.95 per book (includes postage, handling, and tax) for orders of ten.

Visions International Publishing   Ph. (403) 436-1798
P.O. Box 4072
Edmonton, Alberta
Canada, T6E 4S8

Make cheques payable to Visions International Publishing

Name _____

Street _____

City_____Province/State _____

Postal Or Zip Code _____

The Joy Of Not Working

Corporate Purchases

The Joy Of Not Working has helped many individuals see hope and opportunity during retirement and layoffs where before they saw despair and dissatisfaction. This outstanding resource to help your employees create productive lives away from the workplace is available at special prices for quantity purchases.

The Joy Of Not Working is also the perfect gift for your clients who are retiring, unemployed, or overworked. One USA financial organization purchased 500 autographed copies to help clients achieve happiness and satisfaction in retirement.

For more information on prices for orders of over 10 copies, please call Ernie Zelinski at (403) 434-9202.

To order single copies on your credit card by telephone: Call toll free 1-800-265-4559 in Canada and 1-800-356-9315 in USA

To order <u>autographed</u> copies of *The Joy Of Not Working* by mail, send $19.95 per book postpaid (includes postage, handling, and tax). Send $14.95 per book postpaid (includes postage, handling, and tax) for orders of ten.

Visions International Publishing   Ph. (403) 436-1798
P.O. Box 4072
Edmonton, Alberta
Canada, T6E 4S8

Make cheques payable to Visions International Publishing

Name _____

Street _____

City_____Province/State _____

Postal Or Zip Code _____

What They Are Saying About
The Joy Of Not Working

☆ "If you come to work one morning to find a copy of *"The Joy Of Not Working"* on your desk, it probably means you're about to lose your job. If you get up Christmas morning to find a copy under the tree, it could mean you're working too hard. If you buy a copy yourself, you might be wondering if it is possible to find success and satisfaction away from the treadmill."

> *- Michael Kane, Business Reporter, Vancouver Sun*

☆ "Zelinski covers it all: combating boredom, developing motivation, a healthy attitude, living for now, passion, real wants, re-thinking your financial independence and not allowing age to interfere with a fulfilling life."

> *- Bea Smith, Kelowna Courier*

☆ "Dear Mr. Zelinski: When I saw your book *"The Joy Of Not Working"* in Training Magazine, it had great interest to me in preparation for my retirement. I was not disappointed. Both my wife and I have thoroughly read your book and received a lot of benefit and good ideas from it. I have also ordered an additional 10 copies of the book to give to some friends who are contemplating retirement, or are retired already."

> *- A. Eugene Bloomwell, Retirement Planner, South Plainfield, New Jersey*

☆ "Enthusiasm is Zelinski's greatest asset, and underlying this humorous and readable book, chock full of cartoons, quotations, and good solid guidance, is a positive and reassuring view of retirement from one who has been there."

> *- Judy Wayland, Assistant Editor, Good Times - The Canadian Magazine For Successful Retirement*

☆ "Zelinski presents some compelling arguments for taking a close look at who we are, why we work, and whether we really know how to use the leisure time we have."

> *- Sheila McGovern, Workplace Columnist, Montreal Gazette*

☆ "All of us on the consulting team and many of our clients have found *The Joy Of Not Working* has lots of inspiration for working better too."

> *- Bob McCartney, Senior Consultant, Career Transition Management Group, Morgan & Banks Consultants, Sydney, Australia*